Stockport College Learning Centre

D1138122

revised edition, including new recipes

Healthy Heart
COOKBOOK
light low-fat and delicious

J

GE
RE

THE AUSTRALIAN
Women's Weekly

122754

STOCKPORT COLLEGE
LEARNING CENTRE
346006689
LRS1101   08·08·06
4WK   641·5638
122754   TOM

contents

Taking care of your heart is probably the single most important thing you can do for your body and eating a healthy diet is an essential part of that care, along with keeping fit. Full of flavour, our recipes follow the Heart Foundation's guidelines for healthy eating, providing for varied meals covering all the important food groups, keeping saturated fat and salt to a minimum and happily proving "good food" can actually taste good too.

Pamela Clark

Food Director

eating for a healthy heart

A healthy diet can play a major part in preventing heart disease, but if you think that eating healthy food involves endless lettuce and a sense of deprivation, you're in for a pleasant surprise!

a varied diet

Firstly, you should try to eat as wide a range of nutritious food as possible, across all of the major food groups. This will ensure that you get all the different nutrients your body needs and, just as importantly, your meals will be interesting and varied so that eating remains enjoyable.
Of course, there are some foods that you should eat less of than others, but to be realistic, you should think in terms of moderation rather than denying a particular food altogether. This means that you should try to eat lots of breads, cereals, vegetables and fruit, moderate amounts of lean meat, fish and dairy products, and much smaller amounts of sugar, saturated fat and salt.

fat and heart disease

Eating more kilojoules than you use is the major cause of weight gain. Too much fat can contribute to weight gain, and being overweight can significantly increase your risk of heart disease. Saturated fat in particular also has a tendency to raise blood cholesterol levels. Cholesterol, a white, fatty, waxy substance, is produced naturally in the body, but too great a level of cholesterol in the blood can narrow and block arteries, leading to a heart attack or stroke.
Most of us eat more saturated fat than we actually *need* and eating less saturated fat is one of the best things you can do for your health. A certain amount of unsaturated fat is essential to maintain good health. The Heart Foundation recommends that you concentrate on eating the right type of fat – not no fat! No more than 8% of your total daily kilojoules should come from saturated fat. Saturated fat should be replaced with polyunsaturated fats: 8-10% of your total daily kilojoules should come from polyunsaturated fats. Some saturated fat should also be replaced with monounsaturated fats. If you want to calculate the amount and type of fat you are eating, buy a small Fat Counter from a chemist or newsagent.
Saturated fats, which tend to raise blood cholesterol levels, are found mostly in animal products, such as butter, cream, fat on meat, chicken skin, cheese, lard and dripping. Coconut, palm oil, commercially made biscuits, pastries and some snack foods also contain saturated fat. Read food labels carefully: just because a product contains "vegetable oils" does not mean it is an unsaturated fat. Palm oil, for instance, is 50% saturated.
There is also a small class of fats called **trans-fatty acids** which raise cholesterol levels. They occur in dairy products, commercial frying oils and some margarines – when buying margarine, look for one with less than 1% trans-fatty acids.
Polyunsaturated fats, which can help to lower blood cholesterol levels, are found mostly in nuts, grains and seeds, such as sunflower, safflower, soy bean, cottonseed, maize, sesame and grape seed. Oily fish (herring, salmon, tuna, mackerel and sardines) and seafood also contain a particular type of polyunsaturated fats, known as omega-3 fatty acids. These play an important role in protecting the body from heart disease and a healthy diet should include a serve of fish at least 2-3 times a week.
Monounsaturated fats help to lower blood cholesterol levels and are found in olives, olive oil, canola oil, peanuts, peanut oil, avocados, hazelnuts and macadamias.

eat less ... saturated fat

Reducing the saturated fat in your diet does not mean reducing the flavour. By changing a few basic habits you'll be amazed at how much saturated fat you can eliminate from your daily meals without needing to compromise on taste.

• Avoid fried takeaway food, as well as commercial cakes and biscuits – better still, demand they be cooked in healthier fats!

• Eat smaller portions of lean meat (trim any visible fat), remove skin from chicken and increase your intake of fish, including canned fish.

• Fruit, vegetables, breads and cereals should form the major part of your diet. These foods contain dietary fibre and antioxidants, both of which play a role in the prevention of heart disease, as well as cancer.

• Replace high-fat dairy products with lower-fat alternatives and use polyunsaturated or monounsaturated spread on bread or toast.

• Always *measure* the amount of oil you add to a pan, rather than adding a slurp by guesswork, and heat the pan first, before adding oil – it will spread further, so you need less.

• Buy mayonnaise and salad dressings that are low in fat or fat-free.

• Cooking-oil spray is great for saving on added fat – just a light spray will prevent food from sticking.

• Use fillo pastry sheets instead of puff or shortcrust pastry. Coat fillo sheets lightly with cooking-oil spray or water between layers.

• Buy non-stick pans for cooking and use baking paper to line baking dishes, oven trays and cake pans.

• Prepare casseroles and soups a day ahead and refrigerate so that any fat solidifies on the surface and can be skimmed off before reheating.

a healthy lifestyle

Healthy eating is an important step in reducing your risk of heart disease. The Heart Foundation also recommends the following guidelines for a healthier lifestyle:

• Keep within a healthy weight range; check with your doctor.

• Cut down on your salt intake. Too much salt can contribute to high blood pressure which increases the risk of heart disease.

• Drink less alcohol. If you enjoy a drink, there is no need to give it up but be moderate. Excessive amounts of alcohol can lead to weight increase, high blood pressure and other serious disease.

• Do not smoke. The relationship between smoking and heart disease is now too well documented to ignore.

• Take more physical activity. Even gentle physical activity in short periods is beneficial, and certainly better than just thinking about it! There are lots of easy and enjoyable ways to increase your level of activity, and your body will love you for it!

breakfasts, snacks and lunches

Even if you're in a hurry, it's very important not to skip meals, especially breakfast and lunch. Not only do regular small meals and healthy snacks help to keep up your energy levels throughout the day, they also help to avoid the temptation of junk food when you suddenly realise you're starving!

toasted muesli

PREPARATION TIME 15 MINUTES
COOKING TIME 45 MINUTES (plus cooling time)

- 1 cup rolled oats (90g)
- 1/4 cup unprocessed bran (15g)
- 1/4 cup finely chopped dried apricots (35g)
- 1/4 cup finely chopped dried apples (20g)
- 2 tablespoons sultanas
- 1 tablespoon honey
- 1 tablespoon water
- 1 cup skim milk (250ml)

1 Combine oats, bran and fruit in medium bowl; stir in combined honey and water.

2 Spread mixture onto oven tray; bake in slow oven for about 45 minutes or until toasted, stirring occasionally. Cool.

3 Serve muesli with milk, and fresh fruit, if desired.

SERVES 2

per serving 4.4g fat; 1433kJ

store Muesli can be refrigerated in an airtight container for several weeks.

blueberry muffins

PREPARATION TIME 10 MINUTES
COOKING TIME 20 MINUTES

- cooking-oil spray
- 1 cup white self-raising flour (150g)
- 1 cup wholemeal self-raising flour (160g)
- 1/2 cup firmly packed brown sugar (100g)
- 1 cup fresh or frozen blueberries (150g)
- 2 egg-whites, beaten lightly
- 1/3 cup prepared apple sauce (80ml)
- 3/4 cup skim milk (180ml)

1 Lightly coat a 12-hole muffin pan (1/3-cup capacity) with cooking-oil spray.

2 Sift flours into a large bowl; stir in sugar and blueberries.

3 Stir in egg-whites, sauce and milk until almost combined (do not over-mix); spoon into prepared pan.

4 Cook in a hot oven about 20 minutes or until cooked when tested.

MAKES 12 MUFFINS

per muffin 0.5g fat; 545kJ

store Muffins can be made a day ahead and kept in an airtight container at room temperature, or frozen.

roast garlic mushrooms with crispy ham

PREPARATION TIME 10 MINUTES • COOKING TIME 25 MINUTES

200g button mushrooms
150g flat mushrooms, halved
100g Swiss brown mushrooms
1 medium red onion (170g),
  sliced thinly
1 clove garlic, crushed
1 tablespoon lemon juice
coarsely ground black pepper
cooking-oil spray
200g shaved light leg ham
1/2 small French stick,
  sliced thickly
8 basil leaves, torn

1 Combine mushrooms, onion, garlic, lemon juice and pepper in baking dish; spray lightly with cooking-oil spray. Cook in hot oven, uncovered, about 20 minutes or until mushrooms are tender, stirring occasionally.

2 Meanwhile, spread ham on oven tray; cook in hot oven, about 15 minutes or until crisp.

3 Toast bread on both sides; stir basil through mushroom mixture. Serve bread topped with ham and mushroom.

SERVES 2

per serving 5.2g fat; 1103kJ

store Cook recipe just before serving.

mini spinach frittata

PREPARATION TIME 10 MINUTES • COOKING TIME 20 MINUTES

250g baby spinach leaves
1/2 teaspoon olive oil
1 small brown onion (80g),
  sliced thinly
1 tablespoon water
pinch ground nutmeg
2 egg whites
2 tablespoons skim milk
1/2 teaspoon olive oil, extra

1 Steam or microwave spinach until tender. Drain; chop roughly.

2 Heat oil in medium non-stick saucepan; cook onion and the water. Cover; cook until onion is soft. Combine spinach, onion mixture, nutmeg, egg whites and milk in bowl.

3 Lightly grease four egg rings with a little of the extra oil; heat remaining extra oil in large non-stick frying pan. Place egg rings in pan; fill with egg mixture.

4 Cook until mixture is set; remove egg rings. Turn frittata; cook frittata until lightly browned underneath. Serve with a green salad, if desired.

SERVES 2

per serving 0.8g fat; 194kJ

store Cook recipe just before serving.

buttermilk pancakes with golden pears

PREPARATION TIME 15 MINUTES • COOKING TIME 25 MINUTES

1 cup self-raising flour (150g)
1 cup buttermilk (250ml)
$1/4$ cup skim milk (60ml)
1 egg white

GOLDEN PEARS
4 corella pears (665g), peeled and halved
$1/4$ cup golden syrup (60ml)
1 cup water (250ml)
1 tablespoon lemon juice
3 teaspoons cornflour
1 tablespoon water, extra

1 Sift flour into large bowl; gradually stir in combined milks to make a smooth batter. Beat egg white until soft peaks form; fold lightly into batter.

2 Pour $1/2$ cup batter mixture into heated large non-stick frying pan. When bubbles appear, turn pancake; cook until lightly browned underneath. Remove from pan; keep warm. Repeat with remaining batter. Serve pancakes with pears and syrup.

Golden pears Place pears into medium saucepan with golden syrup, the water and juice. Bring to boil; simmer, uncovered, until pears are just tender. Remove pears from syrup; reserve syrup. Stir blended cornflour and the extra water into reserved syrup; stir over heat until mixture boils and thickens.

SERVES 4

per serving 1.9g fat; 1379kJ
store Cook recipe just before serving.

lentil vegetable soup

PREPARATION TIME 15 MINUTES • COOKING TIME 30 MINUTES

1 teaspoon olive oil
1 clove garlic, crushed
1 small brown onion (80g),
  chopped finely
2 small carrots (140g),
  chopped finely
2 trimmed sticks celery (150g),
  chopped finely
1/2 cup red lentils (100g)
1 1/2 cups water (375ml)
1 1/2 cups chicken stock (375ml)
1 bay leaf
1/2 x 410g can no-added-
  salt tomatoes
2 teaspoons no-added-salt
  tomato paste
1 tablespoon finely chopped
  fresh parsley

1 Heat oil in large saucepan; cook garlic, onion, carrot and celery, until onion is soft.

2 Stir in lentils, the water, stock, bay leaf, undrained crushed tomatoes and paste. Bring to boil; simmer, covered, for about 20 minutes or until lentils are soft.

3 Discard bay leaf. Sprinkle with parsley just before serving.

SERVES 2

per serving 3.9g fat; 936kJ

store Soup can be made 2 days ahead and refrigerated, covered, or frozen.

red capsicum soup

PREPARATION TIME 15 MINUTES • COOKING TIME 35 MINUTES

1 large red capsicum
  (350g), halved
1/2 teaspoon olive oil
1 small brown onion (80g),
  chopped finely
1 cup chicken stock (250ml)
1/2 x 250ml carton
  vegetable juice
1 cup water (250ml)
1/2 teaspoon sugar
1/4 cup low-fat plain
  yogurt (60ml)
1 teaspoon chopped fresh chives

1 Cook capsicum, skin side up, under hot grill until skin blisters; peel away skin and chop capsicum.

2 Heat oil in large saucepan; cook onion and capsicum, until onion is soft. Stir in stock, juice and the water. Bring to boil; simmer, covered, for about 20 minutes or until capsicum is soft.

3 Blend or process mixture until smooth; return to pan. Stir in sugar; stir until heated through. Serve soup drizzled with yogurt and sprinkled with chives.

SERVES 2

per serving 0.8g fat; 453kJ

store Soup can be made 2 days ahead and refrigerated, covered.

dips

spicy tomato salsa

PREPARATION TIME 10 MINUTES
COOKING TIME 15 MINUTES (plus cooling time)

4 medium tomatoes (760g), chopped finely
2 cloves garlic, crushed
1 small brown onion (80g), sliced thinly
1 teaspoon Cajun seasoning
2 teaspoons no-added-salt tomato paste

Combine tomatoes with remaining ingredients in small saucepan. Cook, stirring, about 15 minutes or until onion is soft and sauce has thickened; cool.

SERVES 4

per serving 0.4g fat; 153kJ

store Salsa can be made 3 days ahead and refrigerated, covered.

baba ghanoush

PREPARATION TIME 10 MINUTES (plus refrigeration time)
COOKING TIME 35 MINUTES (plus cooling time)

2 small eggplants (460g)
1/3 cup low-fat plain yogurt (80ml)
1 tablespoon lemon juice
2 cloves garlic, crushed
1 teaspoon tahini
1 teaspoon ground cumin
1/2 teaspoon sesame oil
2 tablespoons finely chopped fresh coriander leaves

Halve eggplant lengthways; place on oven tray. Bake in moderately hot oven about 35 minutes or until tender.
Cool; remove and discard skin. Blend or process eggplant with remaining ingredients until smooth. Cover; refrigerate about 30 minutes.

SERVES 4

per serving 2.2g fat; 218kJ

store Baba ghanoush can be made 3 days ahead and refrigerated, covered.

quick beetroot dip

PREPARATION TIME 10 MINUTES

225g can sliced beetroot, drained well
1/4 cup low-fat plain yogurt (60ml)
1 teaspoon ground coriander
2 teaspoons ground cumin

Blend or process all ingredients until smooth.

SERVES 4

per serving 0.6g fat; 137kJ

store Dip can be made 3 days ahead and refrigerated, covered.

Avoid the temptation to snack on junk food high in saturated fat by keeping a supply of bagel chips and healthy dips on hand. Serve them to guests too – they'll never know they're eating low-fat!

bagel chips

PREPARATION TIME 10 MINUTES
COOKING TIME 15 MINUTES
(plus cooling time)

Traditionally, bagels do not contain fat or animal products; these are the correct ones to use for this recipe.

4 bagels
3 teaspoons monounsaturated
   or polyunsaturated oil
2 cloves garlic, crushed
1/2 teaspoon dried
   oregano leaves

1 Using a serrated or electric knife, cut bagels into very thin slices. Place slices in single layer on oven trays; lightly brush one side of each slice with combined oil, garlic and oregano.

2 Bake in moderately slow oven for about 15 minutes or until lightly browned; cool chips on trays.

SERVES 4

per serving 5.3g fat; 1481kJ

store Chips can be stored in an airtight container for a month.

chicken stir-fry with noodles

PREPARATION TIME 15 MINUTES • COOKING TIME 10 MINUTES

250g fresh egg noodles
160g single chicken breast fillet
5cm piece fresh ginger
2 teaspoons olive oil
1 clove garlic, crushed
1 teaspoon sambal oelek
1/2 teaspoon curry powder
1 medium red capsicum (200g),
** sliced thinly**
1 bunch baby bok choy (500g),
** trimmed, halved**
1/2 x 540g can whole baby
** corn, drained**
3 green onions, chopped coarsely
1/2 teaspoon cornflour
1/4 cup water (60ml)
1 tablespoon salt-reduced
** soy sauce**

1 Place noodles in large heatproof bowl; cover with boiling water. Stand 3 minutes; drain.

2 Meanwhile, slice chicken thinly. Cut ginger into thin slices; cut slices into strips.

3 Heat oil in wok or large frying pan; cook chicken, ginger, garlic, sambal and curry powder until fragrant. Add capsicum, bok choy and corn; stir-fry about 3 minutes. Add noodles and onion, stir-fry until heated through.

4 Stir in blended cornflour, water and sauce; stir until mixture boils and thickens.

SERVES 2

per serving 11.4g fat; 1912kJ

store Cook recipe just before serving.

herbed potatoes

PREPARATION TIME 15 MINUTES • COOKING TIME 1 HOUR 20 MINUTES

2 large desiree potatoes (600g)

FILLING
**1 small carrot (70g),
  chopped finely**
75g broccoli, chopped finely
150g reduced-fat ricotta cheese
**1 tablespoon finely chopped
  fresh chives**

1 Wash and dry potatoes. Prick potatoes all over with a skewer; bake in moderate oven for 1 hour.

2 Cut tops off potatoes; scoop out flesh leaving 1cm shell. Reserve flesh.

3 Place shells on oven tray; bake in hot oven for 10 minutes.

4 Spoon filling into shells. Bake in moderate oven for about 10 minutes or until hot. Serve with fresh green salad, if desired.

Filling Boil, steam or microwave carrot and broccoli until soft; drain. Beat cheese in small bowl until smooth; stir in potato flesh, carrot mixture and chives.

SERVES 2

per serving 7.2g fat; 1308kJ

store Cook recipe just before serving.

salmon patties with capsicum yogurt sauce

PREPARATION TIME 20 MINUTES (plus refrigeration and standing time) • COOKING TIME 20 MINUTES

You will need to cook about 2 medium potatoes (400g) for this recipe.

415g can no-added-salt red salmon, drained
1 cup mashed potato (220g)
1 small brown onion (80g), grated coarsely
1/2 teaspoon finely grated lemon rind
1 tablespoon finely chopped fresh chives
1 teaspoon finely chopped fresh dill
1 egg white
1/3 cup polenta (55g), approximately
cooking-oil spray

CAPSICUM YOGURT SAUCE
1 large red capsicum (350g)
1/4 cup no-oil herb and garlic dressing (60ml)
1 teaspoon sugar
1/4 cup low-fat plain yogurt (60ml)

1 Combine salmon, potato, onion, rind, chives, dill and egg white in bowl; mix well. Shape mixture into eight patties; coat with polenta. Refrigerate 30 minutes.

2 Coat patties with cooking-oil spray. Cook patties in heated large non-stick frying pan about 5 minutes on each side or until lightly browned. Serve with capsicum yogurt sauce, and steamed asparagus and zucchini ribbons, if desired.

Capsicum yogurt sauce Quarter capsicum; remove seeds and membrane. Cook under grill or in very hot oven, skin side up, until skin blisters and blackens. Cover capsicum pieces in plastic or paper for 5 minutes. Peel away skin; chop capsicum. Blend or process capsicum, dressing and sugar until smooth; add yogurt. Process until combined.

SERVES 4 (MAKES 8)

per pattie 5.9g fat; 627kJ

store Patties and sauce can be made a day ahead and refrigerated, covered, separately. Uncooked patties may be frozen.

chilli pizza rounds

PREPARATION TIME 10 MINUTES • COOKING TIME 10 MINUTES

**2 tablespoons finely chopped
    fresh oregano**
80g low-fat ricotta cheese
**1 small fresh red chilli, seeded,
    chopped finely**
**1 tablespoon no-added-salt
    tomato paste**
6 slices wholemeal bread (270g)
**2 tablespoons finely grated
    parmesan cheese**
extra oregano leaves

1 Combine oregano, ricotta, chilli and paste in medium bowl.

2 Cut two 5cm rounds from each slice of bread; place rounds under hot grill until lightly browned on both sides.

3 Spread rounds with prepared cheese mixture; sprinkle with parmesan. Place under hot grill for about 5 minutes or until cheese has melted. Sprinkle with extra oregano leaves to serve.

MAKES 12

per pizza 1.7g fat; 277kJ

store Cook recipe just before serving.

vegetable fried rice

PREPARATION TIME 15 MINUTES • COOKING TIME 15 MINUTES

You will need to cook about 1/3 cup (65g) long grain rice for this recipe.

1 clove garlic, crushed
**1 teaspoon finely grated
    fresh ginger**
2 tablespoons water
**1 medium carrot (120g),
    chopped finely**
**1/2 small red capsicum (75g),
    chopped finely**
**2 small zucchini (180g),
    chopped finely**
1 cup cooked long grain rice
**2 tablespoons salt-reduced
    soy sauce**
3 green onions, chopped finely
**2 tablespoons finely chopped
    fresh coriander leaves**

1 Combine, garlic, ginger and the water in wok or large non-stick frying pan; cook over heat until ginger is soft. Add carrot, capsicum and zucchini; cook for 5 minutes. Stir in remaining ingredients; stir over heat until heated through.

SERVES 2

per serving 0.7g fat; 728kJ

store Recipe can be made 3 hours ahead and refrigerated, covered. Reheat gently.

vegetarian spring rolls with sweet and sour sauce

PREPARATION TIME 20 MINUTES • COOKING TIME 35 MINUTES

1 teaspoon polyunsaturated or monounsaturated oil
1 clove garlic, crushed
50g fresh shiitake mushrooms, sliced thinly
2 green onions, sliced thinly
$^1/_4$ medium red capsicum (50g), sliced thinly
2 cups shredded Chinese cabbage (160g)
2 teaspoons salt-reduced soy sauce
6 spring roll wrappers
1 egg white, beaten lightly

SWEET AND SOUR SAUCE
$^1/_2$ cup pineapple juice (125ml)
2 tablespoons white vinegar
1 tablespoon no-added-salt tomato sauce
2 teaspoons brown sugar
1 teaspoon cornflour
1 teaspoon water

1 Heat oil and garlic in large saucepan; cook mushrooms for 2 minutes. Add onion, capsicum and cabbage; cook, covered, until cabbage is wilted.

2 Stir in sauce. Divide mixture between wrappers; fold sides in, roll up.

3 Brush rolls lightly with egg white; place on baking-paper-covered oven tray. Bake in moderately hot oven for about 25 minutes or until lightly browned. Serve with sauce.

Sweet and sour sauce Combine juice, vinegar, sauce and sugar in medium saucepan. Blend cornflour and the water; add to pan. Stir over heat until sauce boils and thickens slightly.

MAKES 6

per roll 1g fat; 181kJ

store Rolls can be prepared 3 hours ahead and refrigerated, covered, before baking.

sandwich fillings

Bored by the same old salad sandwich? Then vary your usual fillings with these tasty low-fat ideas. And why not try a different bread for a change, as well – sandwiches need never be boring again!

curried tuna

1/2 x 185g can tuna in springwater, drained, flaked
1/2 trimmed stick celery (75g), chopped finely
1/2 teaspoon curry powder
1 tablespoon finely chopped fresh parsley leaves
1 tablespoon low-fat coleslaw dressing
4 slices light rye bread (180g)
1 small tomato (130g), sliced thinly

Combine tuna, celery, curry powder and parsley in small bowl. Stir in dressing; mix well. Divide tuna mixture between 2 bread slices; top with tomato and remaining bread.

SERVES 2

per serving 4.7g fat; 1253kJ

store Tuna filling can be made a day ahead and refrigerated, covered.

couscous tabbouleh

2 tablespoons couscous
2 tablespoons boiling water
1/2 cup finely chopped fresh parsley leaves
1 small tomato (130g), seeded, chopped finely
1/2 small red onion (50g), chopped finely
1 tablespoon lemon juice
1 teaspoon finely chopped fresh mint leaves
4 slices black rye bread (210g)
1/2 medium avocado (125g), sliced thinly

Combine couscous and the boiling water in small bowl. Stir with fork until the water is absorbed; cool. Combine couscous, parsley, tomato, onion, juice and mint in bowl. Divide couscous mixture between 2 bread slices; top with avocado and remaining bread.

SERVES 2

per serving 12g fat; 1701kJ

store Tabbouleh can be made a day ahead and refrigerated, covered.

eggplant tahini

1 medium eggplant (300g)
1 tablespoon tahini paste
1 clove garlic, crushed
1 1/2 tablespoons lemon juice
4 slices wholemeal bread (180g)
1 cup coarsely shredded lettuce (80g)
1 tablespoon finely chopped fresh mint leaves

Halve eggplant; place on oven tray. Bake in moderately hot oven for about 25 minutes or until soft; cool. Remove skin; blend or process eggplant, paste, garlic and juice until well combined. You will have about 1 cup of mixture. Spread 2 bread slices each with 2 tablespoons of eggplant mixture. Top with lettuce and mint, then remaining bread. Keep remaining mixture for future use.

SERVES 2

per serving 3.1g fat; 409kJ

store Eggplant mixture can be made 3 days ahead and refrigerated, covered.

chicken celery

200g chicken breast fillet
1 tablespoon lemon juice
1/4 cup low-fat plain yogurt (60ml)
1/4 teaspoon hot English mustard
4 slices wholemeal bread (180g)
1 trimmed stick celery (75g), sliced thinly

Poach, steam or microwave chicken until tender. Cool; slice thinly. Place chicken, juice, yogurt and mustard in medium bowl; stir until combined. Divide chicken mixture between 2 bread slices; top with celery and remaining bread.

SERVES 2

per serving 8.7g fat; 1512kJ

store Chicken mixture can be made a day ahead and refrigerated, covered.

eggplant tahini *(top)*; chicken celery *(bottom)*; couscous tabbouleh and curried tuna *(in background)*

seafood

Low in kilojoules, rich in heart-friendly omega-3 fats, quick to cook and very versatile, fish — including canned varieties — should be on the healthy eating menu at least two or three times a week. But with this collection of delicious seafood recipes, you'll probably want to eat it even more often than that.

fish with paprika and pimiento sauce

PREPARATION TIME 10 MINUTES • COOKING TIME 10 MINUTES

Chargrilled, peeled and sliced red capsicums can be used instead of pimientos.

2 x 200g blue eye fillets
1/2 x 390g can pimientos, drained
1/2 cup firmly packed fresh parsley leaves

PAPRIKA AND PIMIENTO SAUCE
2 teaspoons olive oil
1 small brown onion (80g), chopped finely
1 clove garlic, crushed
2 teaspoons paprika
3/4 cup water (180ml)
2 teaspoons lemon juice
1 teaspoon sugar

1 Poach, steam or microwave fish until tender; drain.

2 Cut half the pimientos into strips; reserve remaining pimientos for sauce.

3 Serve fish on a bed of parsley leaves, topped with sauce and pimiento strips.

Paprika and pimiento sauce Chop reserved pimientos. Heat oil in medium saucepan; cook onion and garlic until soft. Stir in paprika; cook for 30 seconds. Stir in pimientos with remaining ingredients; bring to boil. Simmer, uncovered, for 3 minutes. Blend or process mixture until smooth.

SERVES 2

per serving 11.1g fat; 1303kJ

store Fish is best cooked close to serving time. Sauce can be made a day ahead and refrigerated, covered.

atlantic salmon with herb crumble

PREPARATION TIME 10 MINUTES • COOKING TIME 10 MINUTES

2 x 200g Atlantic salmon fillets
1/3 cup stale white
breadcrumbs (35g)
1 tablespoon lemon juice
1 tablespoon finely chopped
fresh parsley
1 tablespoon finely chopped
fresh chives
1 clove garlic, crushed

1 Cook fish, skin side up, under

hot grill for 5 minutes; turn.

2 Sprinkle with combined breadcrumbs, juice, herbs and garlic; cook for about 5 minutes or until cooked through and lightly browned. Serve with tossed salad, if desired.

SERVES 2

per serving 12.5g fat; 1200kJ

store Cook recipe just before serving.

fish in wine garlic marinade

PREPARATION TIME 10 MINUTES (plus marinating time) • COOKING TIME 20 MINUTES

2 x 250g whole leather jacket fish
1 clove garlic, crushed
1/2 teaspoon finely grated
lemon rind
2 tablespoons lemon juice
1 tablespoon dry white wine
1 teaspoon olive oil
2 teaspoons finely chopped
fresh thyme
1/2 teaspoon finely grated
fresh ginger
1/2 teaspoon sugar

1 Place fish in shallow dish; pour over combined remaining ingredients. Turn fish to coat in marinade; refrigerate for several hours or overnight.

2 Remove fish from marinade; wrap in foil. Place in baking dish; bake in moderate oven for about 20 minutes or until fish are tender. Serve with chargrilled lemon slices, if desired.

SERVES 2

per serving 6.3g fat; 775kJ

store Fish can be marinated a day ahead and refrigerated, covered.

chilli seafood rice

PREPARATION TIME 10 MINUTES • COOKING TIME 25 MINUTES

You will need to cook about 1/3 cup (65g) long grain rice for this recipe.

2 teaspoons polyunsaturated or monounsaturated oil
1 small brown onion (80g), chopped finely
1 clove garlic, crushed
410g can no-added-salt tomatoes
1 small fresh red chilli, chopped finely
1/3 cup dry red wine (80ml)
1 cup cooked long grain rice
1 tablespoon finely chopped fresh parsley
1 small red capsicum (150g), chopped finely
1 small green capsicum (150g), chopped finely
375g white fish fillets, chopped coarsely
100g can crab meat, drained
125g scallops

1 Heat oil in large saucepan; cook onion and garlic until soft.

2 Add undrained, crushed tomatoes, chilli and wine; bring to boil. Boil
   for about 10 minutes or until sauce has thickened.

3 Stir in rice, add parsley, capsicum and seafood; gently stir over heat for
   about 10 minutes or until capsicum is soft and seafood tender.

SERVES 2

per serving 11.9g fat; 2254kJ

store Recipe can be made a day ahead and refrigerated, covered.

seafood casserole with pasta

PREPARATION TIME 15 MINUTES • COOKING TIME 35 MINUTES

Any type of pasta can be used instead of spaghetti.

12 small green prawns (250g)
12 mussels (380g)
2 teaspoons olive oil
1 large brown onion (200g),
  chopped finely
2 cloves garlic, crushed
400g can no-added-salt tomatoes
1/4 cup dry red wine (60ml)
1/4 cup no-added-salt
  tomato paste (60ml)
2 teaspoons brown sugar
2 teaspoons balsamic vinegar
1/4 cup water (60ml)
200g spaghetti
350g flathead fillets, chopped coarsely
250g squid hood, sliced thickly
1 tablespoon coarsely chopped
  fresh oregano
1/3 cup firmly packed basil
  leaves, chopped coarsely

1 Peel and devein prawns leaving tails intact. Clean mussels, discard beard.

2 Heat oil in large saucepan; cook onion and garlic, stirring, until onion is soft. Add undrained crushed tomatoes, wine, paste, sugar, vinegar and the water. Bring to boil; simmer, uncovered, for about 20 minutes or until sauce thickens.

3 Meanwhile, cook spaghetti in large saucepan of boiling water until tender; drain.

4 Add prawns, mussels, fish and squid to tomato sauce; simmer, uncovered, for about 10 minutes or until seafood is cooked through and mussels have opened. Stir in spaghetti, oregano and basil just before serving.

SERVES 4

per serving 11g fat; 2334kJ

store Tomato sauce can be made a day ahead, and refrigerated, covered, or frozen. Add seafood when reheating.

fish fillets with coriander chilli sauce

PREPARATION TIME 10 MINUTES • COOKING TIME 25 MINUTES

6 x 70g ocean perch fillets
1 small brown onion (80g), sliced thinly
1/2 cup water (125ml)
1/4 cup dry vermouth (60ml)
2 tablespoons lime juice
1 small fresh red chilli, chopped finely
2 tablespoons sugar
1 teaspoon cornflour
1 tablespoon finely chopped fresh
  coriander leaves
1/2 medium red capsicum (100g),
  sliced thinly
2 green onions, cut into 5cm lengths
1/4 cup firmly packed fresh
  coriander leaves, extra

1 Place fish in shallow ovenproof dish; top with brown onion. Pour over combined water, vermouth and 1 tablespoon of the juice; cover. Bake in moderate oven for about 15 minutes or until fish is tender.

2 Remove fish; keep warm. Strain and reserve liquid.

3 Place reserved liquid, chilli, sugar and combined cornflour and remaining juice in small saucepan.

4 Stir over heat until sugar dissolves. Bring to boil; simmer until mixture thickens. Stir in chopped coriander. Arrange fish, capsicum, green onion and coriander leaves on serving plate; drizzle with sauce.

SERVES 2

per serving 4.8g fat; 1453kJ

store Cook recipe just before serving.

salmon and herb souffles

PREPARATION TIME 10 MINUTES • COOKING TIME 25 MINUTES

210g can salmon, drained
1 tablespoon finely chopped fresh chives
1 tablespoon finely chopped fresh parsley
pinch cayenne pepper
1 tablespoon monounsaturated or
**   polyunsaturated margarine**
1 tablespoon plain flour
$^1/_2$ cup skim milk (125ml)
2 egg whites

1 Grease two souffle dishes (1 cup capacity). Combine salmon, herbs and pepper in large bowl; mix well.

2 Heat margarine in medium saucepan; stir in flour. Cook until bubbling; remove from heat. Gradually stir in milk; stir over heat until sauce boils and thickens. Stir sauce into salmon mixture.

3 Beat egg whites until soft peaks form; fold into salmon mixture. Spoon mixture into prepared dishes.

4 Bake in moderate oven for about 20 minutes or until risen and well browned.

SERVES 2

per serving 14.3g fat; 1075kJ

store Cook recipe just before serving.

cantonese steamed ginger snapper

PREPARATION TIME 10 MINUTES • COOKING TIME 30 MINUTES

If snapper is unavailable, use your favourite whole firm-fleshed fish for this recipe.

40g piece ginger
4 small whole snapper (1.2kg)
1/4 cup vegetable stock (60ml)
4 green onions, sliced thinly
1/2 cup tightly packed fresh coriander leaves
1/3 cup salt-reduced light soy sauce (80ml)
1 teaspoon sesame oil

1 Peel ginger; cut into thin strips lengthways, then cut into matchstick-size pieces.

2 Score fish three times both sides; place each fish on a separate large sheet of foil. Sprinkle with ginger and drizzle with half the stock; fold foil loosely to enclose fish.

3 Place fish in large bamboo steamer; steam fish, covered, over wok or large frying pan of simmering water for about 30 minutes or until cooked through.

4 Transfer fish to serving dish; sprinkle with onion and coriander, then drizzle with combined remaining stock, sauce and oil. Serve with steamed broccoli and baby corn, if desired.

SERVES 4

per serving 3.2g fat; 573kJ

store Cook recipe just before serving.

salmon rice paper rolls

PREPARATION TIME 30 MINUTES (plus standing time)

Wasabi is available in both paste and powdered forms. We used the paste but, if you add a few drops of cold water to the powder, as instructed on the label, you can use this mixture as a substitute.

50g rice vermicelli
250g thin fresh asparagus spears
12 x 22cm-round rice paper sheets
1/3 cup light sour cream (80ml)
2 teaspoons finely chopped fresh dill
1/4 teaspoon wasabi
2 teaspoons finely grated lemon rind
400g thinly sliced smoked salmon
1 small red onion (100g), sliced finely
60g snow pea sprouts

1 Place vermicelli in medium heatproof bowl; cover with boiling water. Stand until just tender; drain.

2 Boil, steam or microwave asparagus until just tender; drain. Trim ends. Asparagus should be 15cm long.

3 Place 1 sheet of rice paper in medium bowl of warm water until just softened. Lift from water carefully; place on board.

4 Combine sour cream, dill, wasabi and rind in small bowl.

5 Place 1 slice of salmon on one edge of rice paper, towards the centre. Spread with sour cream mixture, top with 2 asparagus spears, onion, sprouts and vermicelli. Fold rice paper over filling. Roll up to enclose filling; one end will remain open.

6 Repeat with remaining rice paper rounds and filling.

SERVES 4

per roll 4g fat; 452kJ

store Make recipe just before serving.

fish kebabs with chilli sauce

PREPARATION TIME 15 MINUTES (plus marinating time) • COOKING TIME 15 MINUTES

You will need to cook about 1/3 cup (65g) long grain rice for this recipe.

300g tuna steaks, cut into 3cm pieces
1 tablespoon salt-reduced soy sauce
1 clove garlic, crushed
1/4 teaspoon grated fresh ginger
1 medium red capsicum (200g), chopped coarsely
1 medium green capsicum (200g), chopped coarsely
2 teaspoons monounsaturated or polyunsaturated oil
1 cup cooked long grain rice

CHILLI SAUCE

1 small fresh red chilli, chopped finely
2 cloves garlic, crushed
1 tablespoon finely chopped fresh coriander leaves
1 tablespoon fish sauce
1 tablespoon lime juice
1 1/2 tablespoons brown sugar
1 tablespoon mirin
1/3 cup water (80ml)

1 Combine fish with sauce, garlic and ginger in large bowl; refrigerate for 1 hour.

2 Thread fish and capsicum alternately onto 4 skewers. Brush with oil; cook under hot grill until fish is tender. Serve kebabs on rice topped with sauce.

Chilli sauce Grind chilli, garlic and coriander to a smooth paste. Add fish sauce, juice, sugar, mirin and the water. Transfer mixture to small saucepan; stir until sugar is dissolved and sauce heated through.

SERVES 2

per serving 10.8g fat; 1964kJ

store Fish can be marinated a day ahead and refrigerated, covered.

chicken and rabbit

Lean, skinless cuts of chicken and rabbit are excellent sources of protein in a healthy diet and can be prepared in a variety of interesting ways, from hearty and satisfying casseroles to stir-fries that can be on the table in a matter of minutes. Always trim any visible fat from your chosen cut and, if time permits, cook casseroles a day ahead and refrigerate so that any solidified fat can be skimmed from the surface and discarded before reheating.

chicken and artichoke parcels

PREPARATION TIME 20 MINUTES • COOKING TIME 25 MINUTES

1/4 **cup dry white wine (60ml)**
1/2 **cup water (125ml)**
1 trimmed stick celery (75g), sliced thinly
1 small brown onion (80g), chopped finely
300g single chicken breast fillet, chopped finely
1 tablespoon plain flour
1/2 **cup skim milk (125ml)**
400g can artichoke hearts in brine, drained, cut into quarters
2 tablespoons finely chopped fresh basil
freshly ground black pepper
8 sheets fillo pastry
cooking-oil spray

1 Combine wine, the water, celery, onion and chicken in medium saucepan; bring to boil. Simmer for about 5 minutes or until onion is soft and chicken is tender.

2 Stir in combined flour and milk; stir until mixture boils and thickens. Remove from heat; stir in artichoke and basil. Season with pepper.

3 Cut pastry sheets in half crossways; layer four halves together, brushing lightly with water between each layer. Repeat with remaining pastry sheets. Place one quarter of chicken mixture on one end of pastry; fold in sides. Roll to enclose filling. Repeat with remaining chicken mixture and pastry.

4 Place parcels on baking-paper-lined oven tray; spray with cooking-oil spray. Bake, uncovered, in moderately hot oven about 15 minutes or until pastry is browned lightly. Serve with mesclun salad, if desired.

MAKES 4

per parcel 5.2g fat; 1074kJ

store Parcels can be prepared a day ahead and refrigerated, covered. Uncooked parcels may be frozen.

honeyed chicken stir-fry

PREPARATION TIME 10 MINUTES (plus marinating time) • COOKING TIME 15 MINUTES

**600g chicken breast fillets,
  sliced thinly**
**2 tablespoons salt-reduced
  soy sauce**
1/4 cup honey (60ml)
1 clove garlic, crushed
**1 teaspoon finely chopped
  fresh ginger**
**100g shiitake mushrooms,
  sliced thinly**
**1 medium red capsicum
  (200g), chopped finely**
**160g snake beans, cut into
  8cm lengths**
425g can baby corn, drained

1 Combine chicken, sauce, honey, garlic and ginger in large bowl; refrigerate for several hours or overnight.

2 Stir-fry mixture in batches in heated wok or large non-stick frying pan until chicken is tender; remove mixture from wok. Add mushroom, capsicum, beans and corn to wok; stir-fry for about 5 minutes or until beans are just tender.

3 Stir in chicken; cook, stirring, for about 2 minutes or until chicken is hot.

SERVES 4

per serving 9.1g fat; 1488kJ

store Cook recipe just before serving.

herb coated chicken

PREPARATION TIME 20 MINUTES • COOKING TIME 30 MINUTES

1 cup stale breadcrumbs (70g)
1 clove garlic, crushed
1/2 teaspoon Cajun seasoning
1 teaspoon finely chopped
fresh thyme
1 teaspoon finely chopped
fresh oregano
2 teaspoons finely chopped
fresh basil
cooking-oil spray
6 chicken tenderloins (270g)
1/3 cup low-fat plain
yogurt (80ml)

1 Combine breadcrumbs, garlic, seasoning and herbs in medium bowl.

2 Lightly spray oven tray with cooking-oil spray. Coat chicken in yogurt, then breadcrumb mixture; place on prepared tray. Cook chicken in moderate oven for about 30 minutes or until lightly browned and cooked through.

3 Serve chicken with tomato, cucumber and snow pea sprout salad with freshly squeezed lemon juice, if desired.

SERVES 2

per serving 9.7g fat; 1466kJ

store Cook recipe just before serving.

grilled tandoori chicken

PREPARATION TIME 10 MINUTES (plus marinating time)
COOKING TIME 15 MINUTES

$1/2$ **cup low-fat plain yogurt (125ml)**
1 tablespoon lemon juice
$1/2$ **teaspoon finely grated fresh ginger**
1 clove garlic, crushed
$1/2$ **teaspoon caster sugar**
$1/2$ **teaspoon paprika**
$1/4$ **teaspoon ground cumin**
$1/4$ **teaspoon ground coriander**
$1/4$ **teaspoon ground turmeric**
pinch chilli powder
2 x 200g single chicken breast fillets

TOMATO, RED ONION AND CORIANDER SALSA
1 small tomato (130g), chopped finely
$1/2$ **small red onion (50g), chopped finely**
1 teaspoon sugar
1 tablespoon finely chopped fresh coriander leaves

1 Combine yogurt, juice, ginger, garlic, sugar, paprika and spices in large bowl. Add chicken; turn chicken to coat in marinade. Refrigerate for several hours or overnight.

2 Grill chicken, brushing with marinade, until browned on both sides and tender. Serve chicken sliced thickly, with tomato, red onion and coriander salsa, and steamed rice, if desired.

Tomato, red onion and coriander salsa Combine all ingredients in small bowl.

SERVES 2

per serving 12.5g fat; 1457kJ

store Chicken is best marinated a day ahead and refrigerated, covered.

ginger chicken kebabs

PREPARATION TIME 15 MINUTES (plus marinating time) • COOKING TIME 15 MINUTES

**300g chicken breast fillets,
   chopped coarsely**
1 tablespoon green ginger wine
**1 tablespoon salt-reduced
   soy sauce**
1 tablespoon lemon juice
**1 teaspoon monounsaturated or
   polyunsaturated oil**
2 teaspoons Worcestershire sauce
2 teaspoons brown sugar
1 teaspoon Dijon mustard
1 teaspoon grated fresh ginger

1 Combine chicken and remaining ingredients in large bowl; refrigerate for several hours or overnight.

2 Thread chicken onto skewers; reserve marinade. Grill kebabs, brushing with marinade, until chicken is tender. Serve sprinkled with sliced green onions, if desired.

SERVES 2

per serving 10.6g fat; 1091kJ

store Chicken is best marinated a day ahead and refrigerated, covered.

spicy thai-style chicken

PREPARATION TIME 10 MINUTES • COOKING TIME 20 MINUTES

500g lean minced chicken
3 cloves garlic, crushed
**1/3 cup mild sweet chilli
   sauce (80ml)**
1 tablespoon fish sauce
**2 tablespoons salt-reduced
   soy sauce**
4 green onions, chopped finely
**2 tablespoons finely shredded
   fresh basil leaves**
500g baby bok choy, halved

1 Cook chicken in heated wok or large non-stick frying pan, stirring, until cooked through.

2 Add garlic and chilli sauce; cook, stirring, until mixture is browned. Stir in sauces, onion and basil.

3 Meanwhile, boil, steam or microwave bok choy until tender; drain.

4 Serve chicken immediately, with bok choy.

SERVES 4

per serving 7.8g fat; 908kJ

store Cook recipe just before serving.

hearty rabbit stew

PREPARATION TIME 15 MINUTES
COOKING TIME 1 HOUR 15 MINUTES

2 teaspoons olive oil
6 spring onions
400g rabbit pieces
1 tablespoon plain flour
$^3/_4$ cup water (180ml)
$^1/_2$ cup dry white wine (125ml)
2 teaspoons no-added-salt tomato paste
4 baby potatoes (270g), quartered
175g baby carrots, trimmed
60g sugar snap peas

1 Heat half of the oil in large saucepan. Cook onions, stirring, for about 3 minutes or until brown all over; set aside.

2 Toss rabbit in flour. Heat remaining oil in pan; cook rabbit until browned all over.

3 Stir in the water, wine and paste; bring to boil. Simmer, covered, for 45 minutes.

4 Add potato and onion; cook for 15 minutes. Add carrot and peas; cook until vegetables are tender.

SERVES 2

per serving 9.2g fat; 1667kJ

store Recipe can be made a day ahead and refrigerated, covered.

rabbit and tomato vegetable casserole

PREPARATION TIME 10 MINUTES • COOKING TIME 1 HOUR

400g rabbit pieces
1 large brown onion (200g),
  chopped finely
200g pumpkin, chopped coarsely
1/2 medium red capsicum (100g),
  chopped finely
410g can no-added-salt tomatoes
1 clove garlic, crushed
1/2 cup dry white wine (125ml)
1/2 cup water (125ml)
2 tablespoons coarsely chopped
  fresh parsley

1 Cook rabbit in heated large non-stick saucepan until browned all over. Add onion; cook, stirring, until onion is soft.

2 Add remaining ingredients, except parsley, to pan; bring to boil. Simmer, covered, for about 45 minutes or until rabbit is tender. Sprinkle with parsley to serve.

SERVES 2

per serving 5.12g fat; 1308kJ

store Recipe can be made a day ahead and refrigerated, covered.

chicken and lentil cacciatore

PREPARATION TIME 15 MINUTES • COOKING TIME 40 MINUTES

cooking-oil spray
8 skinless chicken thigh
fillets (880g), halved
1 medium brown onion (150g),
chopped finely
300g button mushrooms, halved
1 clove garlic, crushed
2 x 440g cans no-added-
salt tomatoes
1 tablespoon no-added-salt
tomato paste
1 cup chicken stock (250ml)
1/3 cup red lentils (65g)
1/2 cup seeded black olives (60g)
1 tablespoon drained capers
2 teaspoons finely chopped
fresh oregano
2 tablespoons finely chopped
fresh parsley

1 Lightly spray large non-stick saucepan with cooking-oil spray. Cook chicken until browned all over, turning occasionally. Remove from pan.

2 Add onion, mushroom and garlic to pan; cook, stirring, until onion is soft. Add undrained crushed tomatoes, paste, stock and lentils.

3 Return chicken to pan; simmer, covered, for about 30 minutes or until chicken is tender. Stir in olives, capers, oregano and parsley.

SERVES 4

per serving 17.3g fat; 1858kJ

store Recipe can be made a day ahead and refrigerated, covered, or frozen.

vegetables

Vegetables play a vital role in any healthy eating plan, being packed with essential nutrients and fibre and almost invariably low in fat. Don't serve them merely as accompaniments – these delicious recipes show just how tasty and satisfying a vegetarian meal can be.

herbed ratatouille with pasta

PREPARATION TIME 10 MINUTES • COOKING TIME 20 MINUTES

1 teaspoon olive oil
1 clove garlic, crushed
1 medium brown onion (150g), chopped coarsely
1 medium eggplant (300g), chopped coarsely
3 medium zucchini (360g), chopped coarsely
1 medium green capsicum (200g), chopped coarsely
2 medium tomatoes (380g), chopped coarsely
1 tablespoon dry red wine
1/3 cup water (80ml)
1 tablespoon no-added-salt tomato paste
2 tablespoons coarsely chopped fresh basil
300g pasta

1 Heat oil in large non-stick saucepan; cook garlic and onion until soft.

2 Stir in eggplant; cook until eggplant is soft. Remove from pan; drain on absorbent paper.

3 Cook zucchini and capsicum separately, following same method as eggplant. Return vegetables with tomato, wine, the water and paste to pan; cook for 5 minutes or until mixture is heated through. Stir through basil just before serving.

4 Add pasta to large saucepan of boiling water; boil, uncovered, until just tender. Drain; serve with ratatouille.

SERVES 2

per serving 6g fat; 2829kJ
store Ratatouille can be made a day ahead and refrigerated, covered.

zucchini lentil pasties

PREPARATION TIME 20 MINUTES (plus refrigeration time) • COOKING TIME 40 MINUTES (plus cooling time)

1 cup plain wholemeal flour (160g)
50g polyunsaturated or
   monounsaturated margarine
1/4 cup cold water
   (60ml), approximately
1 medium brown onion (150g),
   chopped finely
2 cloves garlic, crushed
1 teaspoon curry powder
1/2 teaspoon grated fresh ginger
1/4 teaspoon sambal oelek
1/4 cup red lentils (50g)
2/3 cup water (160ml), extra
1 medium zucchini (120g),
   grated finely
1 egg white

CHILLI AND CORIANDER SAUCE

2 large tomatoes (500g),
   chopped coarsely
1/4 cup water (60ml)
1/3 cup lime juice (80ml)
1/4 cup brown sugar (50g)
1 teaspoon fish sauce
1/3 cup sweet chilli sauce (80ml)
2 tablespoons finely chopped
   fresh coriander leaves

1 Place flour and chopped margarine in food processor; process until combined. With motor operating, add enough of the water until mixture just forms a ball. Lightly knead on a floured surface until smooth; cover. Refrigerate for 20 minutes.

2 Meanwhile, cook onion, garlic, curry powder, ginger and sambal oelek in large non-stick saucepan for 1 minute; stir in lentils and the extra water. Bring to boil; simmer, uncovered, for about 10 minutes or until all liquid is absorbed. Remove from heat; stir in zucchini.

3 Roll pastry out on floured surface until 5mm thick. Cut out six rounds using 12cm cutter; divide filling between rounds. Brush edges with egg white; fold rounds to enclose filling; pinch edges together to seal. Brush with egg white; place on baking paper-covered oven tray.

4 Bake in moderately hot oven for about 25 minutes or until well browned. Serve with chilli and coriander sauce.

Chilli and coriander sauce Combine tomato, the water, juice, sugar and sauces in medium saucepan; stir over low heat until sugar dissolves. Bring to boil; simmer, uncovered, about 10 minutes or until sauce thickens. Remove from heat, cool; stir in coriander.

MAKES 6

per pasty 8.1g fat; 1016kJ

store Uncooked pasties can be made a day ahead and refrigerated, covered, or frozen.

bean and potato bake

PREPARATION TIME 10 MINUTES • COOKING TIME 25 MINUTES

4 small potatoes (480g),
   sliced thinly
2 green onions, sliced thinly
1/2 x 220g can Mexicana
   chilli beans
1/2 cup skim milk (125ml)
1/4 cup grated parmesan
   cheese (20g)

1 Layer potato, onion and beans in two lightly greased ovenproof dishes (1-cup capacity). Pour milk over vegetables; sprinkle with cheese.

2 Bake, uncovered, in moderate oven for about 25 minutes or until vegetables are soft.

SERVES 2

per serving 3.8g fat; 1008kJ

store Cook recipe just before serving.

vegetarian pizza

PREPARATION TIME 20 MINUTES (plus standing time)
COOKING TIME 25 MINUTES

7g sachet (2 teaspoons) dried yeast
$1/2$ teaspoon sugar
$1/2$ cup warm water (125ml)
$1^1/2$ cups plain flour (225g)
1 teaspoon monounsaturated or polyunsaturated oil
$1/4$ cup no-added-salt tomato paste (65g)
$1/2$ cup canned drained red kidney beans (100g)
1 small red onion (100g), sliced thinly
1 small zucchini (90g), sliced thinly
1 small red capsicum (150g), sliced thinly
4 baby mushrooms, sliced thinly
$1/4$ cup grated light mozzarella cheese (25g)
1 tablespoon grated parmesan cheese
1 tablespoon fresh basil leaves

1 Place yeast with sugar in large bowl; stir in the water. Cover; stand in warm place for about 10 minutes or until mixture is frothy.

2 Sift flour into large bowl; stir in yeast mixture and oil. Mix to a firm dough.

3 Turn dough onto floured surface; knead for about 5 minutes or until dough is smooth and elastic.

4 Return dough to bowl; cover. Stand in warm place for about 45 minutes or until doubled in size. Turn dough onto lightly floured surface; knead until smooth.

5 Roll dough large enough to line 20cm pizza tray. Spread dough with paste; top with remaining ingredients, except basil. Bake in moderately hot oven for about 25 minutes or until crust is crisp. Serve pizza with basil leaves sprinkled on top.

SERVES 2

per serving 7.9g fat; 2427kJ

store Uncooked pizza can be prepared 3 hours ahead and refrigerated, covered.

hot vegetable and tofu salad

PREPARATION TIME 15 MINUTES • COOKING TIME 10 MINUTES

1 medium red onion (170g)
3cm piece fresh ginger
2 teaspoons monounsaturated or
   polyunsaturated oil
250g packet firm tofu,
   chopped coarsely
1 small carrot (70g), sliced thinly
1 small red capsicum (150g),
   sliced thinly
100g broccoli, chopped coarsely
100g snow peas
1 trimmed stick celery (75g),
   sliced thinly
1/2 cup vegetable stock (125ml)
2 tablespoons oyster sauce
1 tablespoon salt-reduced
   soy sauce

1 Cut onion into thin wedges. Cut ginger into thin slices; cut slices into thin strips.

2 Heat oil in wok or large non-stick frying pan; cook onion, ginger and tofu until onion is soft and tofu lightly browned.

3 Stir in remaining ingredients; bring to boil. Simmer, uncovered, for about 5 minutes or until vegetables are tender.

SERVES 2

per serving 11.9g fat; 1236kJ

store Cook recipe just before serving.

vegetable risotto

PREPARATION TIME 10 MINUTES (plus standing time) • COOKING TIME 45 MINUTES

1 small eggplant (230g),
   chopped finely
salt
2 teaspoons olive oil
1 small brown onion (80g),
   chopped finely
1 clove garlic, crushed
3/4 cup brown rice (150g)
3/4 cup chicken stock (80ml)
2 cups water (500ml)
2 medium zucchini (240g)
2 medium tomatoes (380g),
   peeled, chopped finely
125g mushrooms, sliced thinly
1/4 cup coarsely grated parmesan
   cheese (20g)
1 tablespoon fresh oregano leaves

1　Place eggplant in colander; sprinkle with salt. Stand for 30 minutes; rinse well under cold water. Pat dry with absorbent paper.

2　Heat oil in large saucepan; cook onion and garlic until soft. Add rice, stock and the water; bring to boil. Simmer, covered, for about 30 minutes or until rice is tender and almost all the liquid is absorbed.

3　Using a vegetable peeler, cut zucchini into ribbons.

4　Stir eggplant, zucchini, tomato and mushroom into rice; cook for about 3 minutes or until vegetables are softened. Stir in half the cheese and oregano; serve risotto sprinkled with remaining cheese.

SERVES 2

per serving　11.2g fat; 1923kJ

store　Risotto best made just before serving.

lentil patties with yogurt mint sauce

PREPARATION TIME 20 MINUTES
COOKING TIME 30 MINUTES (plus cooling time)

$1/2$ **cup red lentils (100g)**
$1/2$ **trimmed stick celery (35g), chopped finely**
1 small carrot (70g), chopped finely
2 cups water (500ml)
$1/2$ **teaspoon ground coriander**
$1/2$ **teaspoon ground cumin**
1 cup stale breadcrumbs (70g)
2 tablespoons plain flour
1 egg white, beaten lightly
1 cup stale breadcrumbs (70g), extra
1 tablespoon finely chopped fresh parsley
1 tablespoon monounsaturated or polyunsaturated oil

YOGURT MINT SAUCE
$1/2$ **cup low-fat plain yogurt (125ml)**
1 tablespoon finely chopped fresh mint
1 small clove garlic, crushed
1 teaspoon lemon juice

1 Combine lentils, celery, carrot, the water, coriander and cumin in large saucepan; bring to boil. Simmer, covered, for about 20 minutes or until mixture is thickened; cool.

2 Stir in breadcrumbs; shape mixture into four patties. Toss in flour; dip in egg white, then combined extra breadcrumbs and parsley.

3 Heat oil in large non-stick frying pan; cook patties until well browned on both sides. Drain on absorbent paper; serve with yogurt mint sauce and a green leaf salad, if desired.

Yogurt mint sauce Combine all ingredients in bowl; mix well.

SERVES 2

per serving 14.3g fat; 2433kJ

store Uncooked patties can be made a day ahead and refrigerated, covered, or frozen.

tasty vegetable pies

PREPARATION TIME 20 MINUTES (plus refrigeration time) • COOKING TIME 35 MINUTES (plus cooling time)

1 cup wholemeal plain
    flour (160g)
50g monounsaturated or
    polyunsaturated margarine
1/4 cup cold water
    (60ml), approximately
20g monounsaturated
    or polyunsaturated
    margarine, extra
1 small leek (200g),
    sliced thinly
2 tablespoons white plain flour
1 cup skim milk (250ml)
1 medium zucchini (120g),
    chopped finely
1 medium carrot (120g),
    chopped finely
1 tablespoon finely chopped
    fresh parsley
1/2 teaspoon skim milk, extra

1 Place wholemeal flour and coarsely chopped margarine in food processor; process until combined. With motor operating, add enough of the water until mixture just forms a ball. Lightly knead on floured surface until smooth. Cover; refrigerate 20 minutes.

2 Heat extra margarine in large saucepan. Stir in leek; cook until soft. Stir in white flour; cook until bubbling.

3 Remove from heat; gradually stir in milk. Stir over heat until sauce boils and thickens. Cover; cool to room temperature.

4 Boil, steam or microwave zucchini and carrot until just tender. Stir vegetables and parsley into sauce. Spoon into two ovenproof dishes (1-cup capacity).

5 Roll pastry out on floured surface until 5mm thick. Cut pastry into two rounds large enough to cover dishes; trim edges. Brush with extra milk; decorate with remaining pastry.

6 Bake in moderately hot oven for about 20 minutes or until pastry is lightly browned and crisp.

SERVES 2

per serving 26.8g fat; 2543kJ

store Uncooked pies can be prepared a day ahead and refrigerated, covered.

curried vegetables

PREPARATION TIME 15 MINUTES • COOKING TIME 25 MINUTES

1/4 cup water (60ml)
1 teaspoon ground cumin
1 teaspoon ground coriander
1 teaspoon garam masala
1 teaspoon curry powder
1 medium brown onion (150g),
    chopped finely
410g can no-added-salt tomatoes
13/4 cups water (430ml), extra
4 baby potatoes (400g), quartered
2 medium carrots (240g),
    chopped finely
300g cauliflower, chopped finely
60g sugar snap peas
375g broccoli, chopped finely
4 small yellow squash
    (200g), halved

1 Heat the water in large saucepan; stir in spices and onion. Simmer until mixture is reduced by half.

2 Add undrained crushed tomatoes, the extra water, potato, carrot and cauliflower. Bring to boil; simmer, covered, for about 10 minutes or until potato is just soft. Add peas, broccoli and squash; simmer, covered, further 5 minutes or until liquid is reduced slightly and vegetables are soft.

SERVES 2

per serving 2.5g fat; 1378kJ

store Curry can be made a day ahead and refrigerated, covered.

64

vegetable moussaka

PREPARATION TIME 10 MINUTES
COOKING TIME 50 MINUTES (plus cooling time)

1 large eggplant (500g), sliced thickly
2 large tomatoes (500g), chopped finely
1 teaspoon sugar
2 teaspoons monounsaturated or polyunsaturated margarine
1 tablespoon plain flour
1 cup skim milk (250ml)
2 tablespoons finely grated parmesan cheese
2 tablespoons finely chopped fresh basil leaves

1 Place eggplant in single layer on oven tray; bake, uncovered, in moderately hot oven for 15 minutes. Turn, bake for further 15 minutes or until browned lightly; cool for 10 minutes.

2 Combine tomato and sugar in small saucepan; cook, stirring occasionally, for about 30 minutes or until tomato is soft and liquid almost evaporated.

3 Meanwhile; melt margarine in small saucepan; add flour. Cook; stirring for 1 minute. Gradually add milk; stir over medium heat until sauce boils and thickens. Stir in half the cheese and half the basil. Stir remaining basil through tomato mixture.

4 Spread one-third of tomato mixture, eggplant and cheese sauce in two ovenproof dishes (2-cup capacity); repeat with two more layers. Sprinkle with remaining cheese.

5 Bake, uncovered, in moderate oven, about 15 minutes or until moussaka is lightly browned.

SERVES 2

per serving 6.1g fat; 867kJ

store Moussaka can be prepared 3 hours ahead and refrigerated, covered.

spicy bean casserole

1/2 cup dried red kidney beans (100g)
1/2 cup dried chick peas (100g)
2 teaspoons monounsaturated or
   polyunsaturated margarine
1 medium red onion (170g),
   sliced thinly
1 medium carrot (120g),
   chopped coarsely
1 small red capsicum (150g),
   chopped finely
1 clove garlic, crushed
1 small fresh red chilli, chopped finely
1 teaspoon ground cumin
1/2 teaspoon ground cinnamon
1/2 teaspoon ground nutmeg
410g can no-added-salt tomatoes
1/2 cup vegetable stock (125ml)
2 teaspoons no-added-salt tomato paste
1/2 cup canned no-added-salt corn
   kernels (100g), drained
2 teaspoons finely chopped
   fresh parsley

1 Cover beans and chick peas with water in small bowl. Stand overnight; drain.

2 Heat margarine in large saucepan; cook onion, carrot, capsicum, garlic and chilli until onion is soft.

3 Stir in cumin, cinnamon and nutmeg; cook for further minute. Stir in beans and chick peas, undrained crushed tomatoes, stock and paste.

4 Bring to boil; simmer, covered, for about 45 minutes, stirring occasionally, or until beans and chick peas are tender. Stir in corn; simmer for further 5 minutes. Sprinkle with parsley just before serving.

SERVES 2

per serving 6.7g fat; 1173kJ

store Recipe can be made a day ahead and refrigerated, covered.

pasta with pesto sauce

2 cups fresh basil leaves (160g)
1 clove garlic, crushed
1/3 cup grated parmesan cheese (25g)
1 tablespoon olive oil
1 tablespoon No Oil Light French Dressing
250g spaghetti pasta

1 Blend or process basil, garlic, cheese, oil and dressing until well combined.

2 Add pasta to large saucepan of boiling water. Boil, uncovered, until just tender; drain.

3 Toss pesto through pasta before serving.

SERVES 2

per serving 15.6g fat; 2512kJ

store Pesto can be made 3 days ahead and refrigerated, covered.

meat

There is no need to avoid red meat when you are eating for a healthy heart — it is a very valuable source of protein and iron. Just remember to choose lean cuts of beef, veal, lamb or pork, trim away all visible fat *before* cooking and serve with lots of fresh vegies for a perfectly balanced meal.

beef and beer casserole

PREPARATION TIME 10 MINUTES • COOKING TIME 1 HOUR

400g lean topside or rump steak
1¹/₂ tablespoons plain flour
2 teaspoons olive oil
1 medium leek (350g), sliced thickly
1 small red capsicum (150g), chopped coarsely
100g button mushrooms
1 medium tomato (190g), peeled, chopped finely
1 cup beer (250ml)
¹/₂ cup water (125ml)
2 teaspoons no-added-salt tomato paste
1 tablespoon finely chopped fresh parsley
2 teaspoons finely chopped fresh oregano leaves

1 Trim all visible fat from steak; cut steak into cubes. Toss steak in flour. Heat oil in large saucepan; cook steak until browned all over. Remove steak from pan.

2 Add leek, capsicum and mushrooms to pan; cook for about 5 minutes or until leek is soft.

3 Add steak, tomato, beer, the water and paste; bring to boil. Simmer, covered, for 40 minutes; remove lid. Simmer for further 10 minutes or until sauce has thickened slightly and meat is tender. Stir in herbs just before serving. Serve with soft polenta or steamed baby potatoes, if desired.

SERVES 2

per serving 14.6g fat; 1863kJ

store Casserole can be made a day ahead and refrigerated, covered.

veal with marsala sauce

PREPARATION TIME 15 MINUTES (plus marinating time) • COOKING TIME 15 MINUTES

4 x 75g veal steaks
1/4 cup marsala (60ml)
1 tablespoon lemon juice
1/2 teaspoon olive oil
1 large carrot (180g)
1 large zucchini (150g)
1 teaspoon cornflour
3/4 cup water (180ml)
1 clove garlic, crushed
3 teaspoons plum jam
3 green onions, sliced thinly

1 Remove all visible fat from veal; pound veal thinly. Combine veal with marsala and juice in bowl; refrigerate for several hours or overnight.

2 Drain veal; reserve marinade. Heat oil in medium non-stick saucepan; cook veal until tender. Remove from pan.

3 Cut carrot and zucchini into 10cm lengths. Cut each piece into thin strips; cut strips into matchstick-size pieces. Boil, steam or microwave until vegetables are tender; keep warm.

4 Blend cornflour with reserved marinade in pan; add the water, garlic and jam. Stir over heat until mixture boils and thickens. Serve veal on a bed of potato mash, if desired. Serve with sauce and top with vegetables and onion.

SERVES 2

per serving 5.2g fat; 1573kJ

store Cook veal just before serving.

beef and onion kebabs

PREPARATION TIME 20 MINUTES (plus marinating time) • COOKING TIME 10 MINUTES

350g lean rump steak
9 baby onions (225g), halved

MARINADE
1/4 cup honey (60ml)
1/4 cup lemon juice (60ml)
2 teaspoons grated fresh ginger
2 teaspoons Worcestershire sauce
1/4 cup no-added-salt
  tomato sauce (60ml)
1 tablespoon finely chopped fresh
oregano leaves

1 Remove all visible fat from steak; chop steak into bite-size pieces. Thread steak and onion onto six skewers.

2 Place kebabs in shallow dish; add marinade. Refrigerate overnight.

3 Cook kebabs on heated grill pan or barbecue, brushing with marinade, until meat is tender. Serve with bitter leaf salad, if desired.

Marinade Combine all ingredients in bowl; mix well.

SERVES 2

per serving 8.3g fat; 1794kJ

store Cook marinated kebabs just before serving.

lemon veal stir-fry with capsicums and pecans

PREPARATION TIME 15 MINUTES • COOKING TIME 15 MINUTES

300g veal steaks
1 medium brown onion (150g), cut into thin wedges
1 medium red capsicum (200g), sliced thinly
1 medium green capsicum (200g), sliced thinly
1 tablespoon finely chopped fresh lemon grass
2 tablespoons pecans, halved
1 teaspoon finely grated lemon rind
2 tablespoons lemon juice
2 tablespoons salt-reduced soy sauce
1 clove garlic, crushed

1 Remove all visible fat from veal. Slice veal thinly. Heat wok or large non-stick frying pan; cook veal until browned all over. Remove veal from wok.

2 Add onion, capsicum and lemon grass to wok; stir-fry until vegetables are soft.

3 Stir in nuts; cook for 1 minute. Stir in veal with combined rind, juice, sauce and garlic; stir-fry until heated through. Serve with stir-fried noodles or steamed rice, if desired.

SERVES 2

per serving 10.3g fat; 1238kJ

store Cook recipe just before serving.

beef in red wine

PREPARATION TIME 15 MINUTES • COOKING TIME 1¹/4 HOURS

350g beef blade steak
2 medium brown onions (300g),
    chopped finely
1 clove garlic, crushed
100g mushrooms, sliced thickly
415ml can tomato puree
2 teaspoons Worcestershire sauce
¹/2 cup dry red wine (125ml)
1 trimmed stick celery (75g),
    chopped coarsely
2 medium carrots (240g),
    chopped coarsely
2 tablespoons fresh parsley leaves

1   Trim all visible fat from steak; cut steak into cubes. Cook steak in heated large non-stick saucepan until browned all over. Add onion, garlic and mushrooms; cook, stirring, for about 2 minutes or until onion is soft. Stir in puree, sauce and wine; bring to boil. Simmer, covered, about 45 minutes.

2   Add celery and carrot; cook, covered, for further 15 minutes or until vegetables are tender. Serve sprinkled with parsley. Serve with couscous, if desired.

SERVES 2

per serving 8g fat; 1708kJ

store Recipe can be made a day ahead and refrigerated, covered.

baked crumbed veal

PREPARATION TIME 10 MINUTES • COOKING TIME 15 MINUTES

4 x 60g veal steaks
2 tablespoons low-fat mayonnaise
¹/2 cup seasoned stuffing
    mix (45g)

1   Remove all visible fat from steaks. Lightly spread each steak with mayonnaise; coat completely with stuffing mix.

2   Place veal on oven tray; bake in hot oven for about 15 minutes or until veal is tender. Serve veal with steamed baby potatoes, sugar snap peas, baby rocket leaves and lemon slices, if desired.

SERVES 2

per serving 6.5g fat; 854kJ

store Recipe can be prepared a day ahead and refrigerated, covered. Cook just before serving.

meatballs in rosemary paprika sauce

PREPARATION TIME 15 MINUTES
COOKING TIME 45 MINUTES

250g lean minced beef
1/2 cup stale breadcrumbs (35g)
1 tablespoon finely chopped fresh parsley
1 tablespoon finely chopped fresh chives
1 egg white
1 teaspoon Worcestershire sauce
1 teaspoon monounsaturated or polyunsaturated oil
250g tagliatelle pasta

ROSEMARY PAPRIKA SAUCE
410g can no-added-salt tomatoes
1 cup water (250ml)
2 tablespoons dry red wine
1 medium brown onion (150g), chopped finely
1/2 teaspoon Worcestershire sauce
1 teaspoon paprika
3 sprigs rosemary

1 Combine mince, breadcrumbs, parsley, chives, egg white and sauce in large bowl. Shape mixture into small meatballs.

2 Heat oil in medium non-stick saucepan; cook meatballs until well browned all over and cooked through. Drain on absorbent paper.

3 Cook pasta in large saucepan of boiling water until tender; drain.

4 Add meatballs to sauce; mix well. Stir until heated through. Serve with pasta, and a crisp green leaf salad, if desired.

Rosemary paprika sauce Combine undrained crushed tomatoes with remaining ingredients in medium saucepan; bring to boil. Simmer, uncovered, for about 20 minutes or until thickened slightly. Remove and discard rosemary sprigs.

SERVES 2

per serving 14.5g fat; 3685kJ

store Recipe can be made a day ahead and refrigerated, covered, or frozen. Cook pasta close to serving.

veal cutlets with tomato basil sauce

PREPARATION TIME 10 MINUTES • COOKING TIME 25 MINUTES

2 x 150g veal cutlets
2 teaspoons olive oil
4 tomatoes (760g), peeled,
 chopped finely
1/2 cup water (125ml)
1 small fresh red chilli,
 chopped finely
1 clove garlic, crushed
2 teaspoons sugar
1 1/2 tablespoons balsamic vinegar
1 tablespoon torn fresh
 basil leaves

1 Remove all visible fat from veal. Heat oil in medium saucepan; cook veal until browned on both sides and tender. Remove veal from pan; keep warm.

2 Add tomatoes, the water, chilli, garlic and sugar to pan; stir over heat for about 10 minutes or until tomatoes are soft and sauce has thickened.

3 Stir in vinegar and basil; cook stirring, for 2 minutes. Serve veal with tomato basil sauce, and roasted kipfler potatoes and steamed baby beans, if desired.

SERVES 2

per serving 7.8g fat; 1017kJ

store Sauce can be made a day ahead and refrigerated, covered. Cook veal just before serving.

peppered veal medallions

PREPARATION TIME 10 MINUTES (plus marinating time) • COOKING TIME 10 MINUTES

4 x 80g veal medallions
2 tablespoons drained canned
  green peppercorns,
  chopped finely
1/4 cup brandy (60ml)
1/2 cup water (125ml)
1 teaspoon cornflour
2 tablespoons light sour cream

1 Remove all visible fat from veal. Combine veal, peppercorns and brandy in medium bowl. Cover; refrigerate for several hours or overnight.

2 Drain veal; reserve marinade. Cook veal in heated large non-stick saucepan until tender. Remove from pan; keep warm.

3 Combine reserved marinade and blended water and cornflour in pan; bring to boil. Remove from heat, stir in cream. Simmer for 5 minutes or until thickened. Pour over veal just before serving. Serve with steamed baby beans, if desired.

SERVES 2

per serving 10.7g fat; 1446kJ

store Cook veal just before serving.

beef and pear with garlic mustard sauce

PREPARATION TIME 10 MINUTES
COOKING TIME 25 MINUTES (plus cooling and standing time)

1 medium pear (230g), quartered
3/4 cup water (180ml)
1/2 cup orange juice (125ml)
350g piece Scotch fillet steak
1/2 teaspoon olive oil
2 cloves garlic, crushed
2 teaspoons seeded mustard
2 teaspoons cornflour
1 tablespoon brandy
1 clove garlic, crushed, extra

1 Combine pear, the water and juice in small saucepan; bring to boil. Remove from heat; cool pear in liquid.

2 Remove all visible fat from steak. Heat oil in medium non-stick saucepan; cook fillet until browned all over. Place fillet in baking dish; cook, covered, in moderate oven for about 20 minutes or until tender. Stand for 5 minutes before slicing.

3 Meanwhile, drain pear, reserving 1$\frac{1}{4}$ cups liquid. Add garlic and mustard to pan; cook for 1 minute. Stir in blended cornflour and reserved liquid; stir over heat until mixture boils and thickens.

4 Stir in brandy and extra garlic. Serve sliced beef with pear and sauce. Serve with wilted spinach and steamed asparagus, if desired.

SERVES 2

per serving 9.9g fat; 1457kJ

store Cook recipe just before serving.

lamb hot pot
with couscous

600g lamb leg chops
1 tablespoon plain flour
2 teaspoons olive oil
1 medium brown onion (150g), cut into thin wedges
1 teaspoon ground cinnamon
1 teaspoon ground turmeric
1 cup water (250ml)
$1/2$ cup beef stock (125ml)
100g prunes, pitted
2 tablespoons finely chopped fresh coriander leaves

COUSCOUS
1 cup boiling water (250ml)
1 cup couscous (200g)

1 Trim all visible fat from lamb. Cut lamb into cubes; toss in flour.

2 Heat oil in large saucepan; cook onion until soft. Add lamb; cook until lamb is browned all over. Stir in cinnamon and turmeric; cook 1 minute.

3 Stir in the water, stock and prunes; bring to boil. Simmer, covered, for about 30 minutes or until lamb is tender. Serve lamb with couscous, sprinkled with coriander.

Couscous Pour the water over couscous in medium bowl; stand for 5 minutes or until liquid is absorbed. Stir with a fork.

SERVES 2

per serving 20.3g fat; 3648kJ

store Hot pot can be made a day ahead and refrigerated, covered. Couscous is best made close to serving time.

lamb fillets in herb vinaigrette

PREPARATION TIME 10 MINUTES
COOKING TIME 10 MINUTES (plus standing time)

300g lamb fillets
2 teaspoons cracked black peppercorns

HERB VINAIGRETTE

2 teaspoons monounsaturated or
polyunsaturated oil
1¹/₂ tablespoons tarragon vinegar
1 tablespoon water
2 teaspoons sugar
1 teaspoon drained canned green peppercorns
¹/₂ teaspoon seeded mustard
2 green onions, chopped finely
2 teaspoons finely chopped fresh parsley
1 teaspoon fresh thyme leaves

1 Trim all visible fat from fillets. Press peppercorns onto fillets.

2 Cook lamb in heated medium non-stick saucepan until tender. Stand, covered, for 5 minutes.

3 Slice lamb; place in large bowl. Gently toss in herb vinaigrette. Serve with thickly sliced egg tomatoes, if desired.

Herb vinaigrette Combine all ingredients in medium bowl; mix well.

SERVES 2

per serving 10.3g fat; 1058kJ

store Recipe can be prepared 3 hours ahead and refrigerated, covered.

lamb and yogurt curry

PREPARATION TIME 10 MINUTES
COOKING TIME 1 HOUR

400g lean diced lamb
1 large brown onion (200g), chopped finely
1 teaspoon finely grated fresh ginger
1 clove garlic, crushed
1 small fresh red chilli, chopped finely
1 teaspoon ground coriander
2 teaspoons ground cumin
¹/₂ teaspoon ground black pepper
1 teaspoon garam masala
2 teaspoons ground turmeric
¹/₄ teaspoon ground cardamom
2 tablespoons lemon juice
1 cup water (250ml)
¹/₂ cup low-fat plain yogurt (125ml)

1 Combine lamb and remaining ingredients, except yogurt, in large saucepan. Simmer, covered, for about 1 hour, or until meat is tender and liquid is reduced by half.

2 Stir in yogurt. Serve with steamed basmati rice and microwaved pappadams, if desired.

SERVES 2

per serving 16g fat; 1670kJ

store Recipe can be made a day ahead and refrigerated, covered, or frozen.

lamb kibbe
with tahini sauce

PREPARATION TIME 15 MINUTES (plus standing time)
COOKING TIME 40 MINUTES

cooking-oil spray
1/2 cup burghul (80g)
500g lean minced lamb
2 small brown onions (100g), chopped finely
2 tablespoons finely chopped pine nuts
2 egg whites
1/3 cup finely chopped fresh parsley
2 tablespoons finely chopped fresh mint leaves

TAHINI SAUCE
1/3 cup low-fat plain yogurt (80ml)
2 teaspoons tahini paste
2 teaspoons salt-reduced soy sauce
2 teaspoons finely chopped fresh parsley

1 Spray deep 20cm round cake pan with cooking-oil spray.

2 Cover burghul with cold water in small bowl; stand for 1 hour. Drain; squeeze out excess moisture.

3 Combine burghul, lamb, onion, nuts, egg whites and herbs in large bowl; press mixture into prepared pan.

4 Bake in moderate oven for about 40 minutes, or until cooked through. Cut into wedges. Serve with tahini sauce, topped with parsley leaves, if desired.

Tahini sauce Combine all ingredients in small bowl; mix well.

SERVES 4

per serving 15.7g fat; 1299kJ

store Lamb kibbe can be made up to 2 days ahead and refrigerated, covered. Sauce can be made 3 hours ahead and refrigerated, covered.

rosemary pork with orange sauce

PREPARATION TIME 10 MINUTES
COOKING TIME 30 MINUTES

You will need two oranges for this recipe.

300g pork fillet
2 teaspoons olive oil
1 tablespoon Grand Marnier
$1/2$ cup chicken stock (125ml)
1 teaspoon cornflour
1 tablespoon water
$1/2$ cup orange juice (125ml)
2 sprigs fresh rosemary

1 Trim all visible fat from pork. Heat oil in medium saucepan; cook pork until browned all over. Place pork on rack in baking dish.

2 Add liqueur and stock to pan; bring to boil. Pour into baking dish.

3 Bake, covered, in moderate oven for about 20 minutes or until pork is tender. Remove pork from rack; keep warm.

4 Stir in combined blended cornflour and water with juice into dish. Stir over heat until mixture boils and thickens; stir in rosemary. Serve pork with sauce. Serve with steamed green and yellow zucchini and torn witlof, if desired.

SERVES 2

per serving 8.4g fat; 1158kJ

store Cook recipe just before serving.

chilli pork and bean feast

PREPARATION TIME 10 MINUTES • COOKING TIME 40 MINUTES

600g pork butterfly steaks
1 teaspoon monounsaturated or
   polyunsaturated oil
1 clove garlic, crushed
1 medium brown onion (150g),
   chopped finely
1 cup water (250ml)
410g can no-added-salt tomatoes
1 tablespoon no-added-salt
   tomato paste
1/2 teaspoon chilli powder
1/2 teaspoon ground cumin
1/2 teaspoon ground coriander
310g can red kidney beans,
   rinsed, drained
1 medium green capsicum (200g),
chopped finely

1 Trim all visible fat from pork (you should have 300g trimmed meat). Blend or process pork until minced.

2 Heat oil in medium saucepan; cook garlic and onion until soft. Stir in pork; stir until browned all over.

3 Stir in the water, undrained crushed tomatoes, paste, chilli, cumin and coriander. Bring to boil; simmer, uncovered, for 30 minutes. Stir in beans and capsicum; stir until heated through. Serve with crisp Lebanese bread wedges, if desired.

SERVES 2

per serving 14.3g fat; 2353kJ

store Recipe can be made 2 days ahead and refrigerated, covered.

pork with port and mushroom sauce

PREPARATION TIME 10 MINUTES • COOKING TIME 15 MINUTES

4 x 100g pork medallions

PORT AND MUSHROOM SAUCE
2 teaspoons monounsaturated or polyunsaturated margarine
100g Swiss brown mushrooms
$^1/_2$ cup beef stock (125ml)
$^1/_2$ cup water (125ml)
1 teaspoon Worcestershire sauce
2 tablespoons port

1 Trim all visible fat from pork. Cook pork in heated large non-stick saucepan for about 3 minutes each side or until cooked through. Serve pork with port and mushroom sauce. Serve with kumara mash and baby rocket leaves, if desired.

Port and mushroom sauce Melt margarine in heated small non-stick saucepan, cook mushrooms, stirring until browned. Add remaining ingredients; bring to boil. Simmer, uncovered, for about 5 minutes or until liquid is reduced by half and sauce has thickened slightly.

SERVES 2

per serving 7.9g fat; 1207kJ

store Cook recipe just before serving.

stir-fried pork and vegetables

PREPARATION TIME 15 MINUTES
COOKING TIME 15 MINUTES

200g pork fillet, sliced thinly
2 teaspoons monounsaturated or polyunsaturated oil
1 small red onion (100g), sliced thickly
400g bok choy, halved lengthways
150g baby green beans
250g fresh asparagus, halved
1 tablespoon black bean sauce
$1/2$ cup water (125ml)
1 tablespoon honey
2 tablespoons salt-reduced soy sauce
1 teaspoon grated fresh ginger
2 teaspoons cornflour

1 Cook pork in heated medium non-stick saucepan, until well browned and tender; remove from pan.

2 Heat oil in same pan; cook onion, stirring, about 1 minute, or until onion is soft. Add bok choy, beans and asparagus; cook, stirring, until vegetables are tender.

3 Stir in combined remaining ingredients; return pork to pan. Stir over high heat until mixture boils and thickens. Serve with steamed jasmine rice, if desired.

SERVES 2

per serving 7.9g fat; 1193kJ

store Cook recipe just before serving.

accompaniments

Using a delicious and interesting range of fresh vegetables, herbs and salad ingredients, these accompaniments show how easy it is to add variety and flavour to a meal, as well as satisfy the heartiest appetite – without loading on unnecessary fat and kilojoules.

mixed vegetables with tarragon vinaigrette

PREPARATION TIME 15 MINUTES • COOKING TIME 10 MINUTES

1/2 **small butternut pumpkin (700g), peeled, chopped coarsely**
6 **baby potatoes (240g), halved**
100g **snow peas**

TARRAGON VINAIGRETTE

2 **teaspoons shredded fresh tarragon**
11/2 **tablespoons white wine vinegar**
2 **teaspoons olive oil**
1/2 **teaspoon cracked black peppercorns**
1/4 **teaspoon sugar**

Boil, steam or microwave pumpkin, potato and snow peas separately until just tender; drain. Combine vegetables in medium bowl; add tarragon vinaigrette.

Tarragon vinaigrette Combine all ingredients in screw-top jar; shake well.

SERVES 2

per serving 5.9g fat; 1041kJ

store Cook recipe just before serving.

beans with asparagus and mushrooms

PREPARATION TIME 10 MINUTES • COOKING TIME 10 MINUTES

75g butter beans
75g baby green beans
75g asparagus, halved
1/2 cup vegetable stock (125ml)
1/2 cup water (125ml)
100g button mushrooms, halved
1 tablespoon fresh coriander leaves

Combine beans, asparagus, stock and the water in large saucepan; bring to boil. Simmer, covered, until vegetables are tender. Stir in mushrooms; simmer, covered, until mushrooms are just tender. Stir in coriander just before serving.

SERVES 2

per serving 0.6g fat; 161kJ

store Cook recipe close to serving time.

honey mustard-glazed kumara

PREPARATION TIME 15 MINUTES • COOKING TIME 35 MINUTES

Kumara is orange coloured sweet potato.

2 large kumara (1kg)
6 baby onions (150g), halved
1/2 cup honey (125ml)
2 tablespoons balsamic vinegar
2 tablespoons seeded mustard
1 tablespoon water
1 tablespoon peanut oil
1 tablespoon grated fresh ginger
50g baby rocket leaves

1 Slice kumara into 1cm rounds. Place kumara and onion in large bowl; toss with combined honey, vinegar, mustard, water, oil and ginger. Drain vegetables; reserve honey-mustard mixture.

2 Place vegetables on wire rack over foil-covered oven tray. Bake in moderately hot oven 35 minutes, brushing frequently during cooking with honey-mustard mixture, until vegetables are browned lightly. Serve kumara with rocket.

SERVES 4

per serving 5.2g fat; 1542kJ
store Cook recipe close to serving time.

dressings

These clever recipes prove that salad dressings can be full of flavour without being full of fat.
Try them on your favourite green salad, coleslaw, or lightly steamed vegetables.

low-fat vinaigrette

PREPARATION TIME 5 MINUTES

3/4 cup No Oil French dressing (180ml)
1 tablespoon olive oil
2 tablespoons coarsely chopped fresh parsley
1/2 teaspoon cracked black peppercorns
1/2 teaspoon sugar
2 teaspoons seeded mustard

Combine all ingredients in screw-top jar; shake well.

MAKES 1 CUP (250ML)

per tablespoon (20ml) 1.6g fat; 113kJ

store Vinaigrette can be made one week ahead and refrigerated, covered.

lemon pepper mayonnaise

PREPARATION TIME 5 MINUTES

1/2 cup low-fat mayonnaise (125ml)
2 teaspoons canned green peppercorns, drained, crushed
1 teaspoon finely grated lemon rind
2 teaspoons lemon juice
1/2 teaspoon sugar

Combine all ingredients in small bowl; mix well.

MAKES 2/3 CUP (160ML)

per tablespoon (20ml) 2.1g fat; 145kJ

store Dressing can be made one week ahead and refrigerated, covered.

guilt-free dressing

PREPARATION TIME 5 MINUTES

1/2 cup buttermilk (125ml)
2 tablespoons finely chopped fresh chives
2 tablespoons No Oil French dressing
1 tablespoon seeded mustard
1 tablespoon honey

Combine all ingredients in screw-top jar; shake well.

MAKES ABOUT 2/3 CUP (160ML)

per tablespoon (20ml) 0.4g fat; 104kJ

store Dressing can be made three days ahead and refrigerated, covered.

(clockwise from left):
guilt-free dressing
low-fat vinaigrette
lemon pepper mayonnaise

confetti coleslaw

1 cup finely shredded cabbage (80g)
1 cup finely shredded red cabbage (80g)
1 small carrot (70g), grated
2 green onions, sliced finely
1 tablespoon low-fat mayonnaise
1 tablespoon water

Combine all ingredients in medium bowl.

SERVES 2

per serving 1.5g fat; 199kJ

store Make recipe just before serving.

parsley salad

$1/4$ cup burghul (40g)
2 cups firmly packed fresh parsley leaves
2 green onions, chopped finely
2 medium tomatoes (380g), seeded,
  chopped finely
1 small red onion (80g), chopped finely
$1/4$ cup finely chopped fresh mint leaves
1 teaspoon finely grated lemon rind
2 tablespoons lemon juice

1 Place burghul in a medium bowl; cover with warm water. Stand 15 minutes.

2 Meanwhile, chop parsley coarsely. Combine parsley, green onion, tomato, red onion and mint in large bowl with rind and lemon juice.

3 Drain burghul, pressing as much water as possible from burghul. Add burghul to parsley mixture; stir through.

SERVES 2

per serving 0.6g fat; 339kJ

store Make salad just before serving.

confetti coleslaw *(above right)*
parsley salad *(below right)*

sweet things

Of *course* you can have the occasional indulgence, and we've chosen these recipes because they allow you to have a treat without doing too much damage to your waistline. Fruit features, naturally, but there are also some wickedly delicious tarts, cakes, biscuits and heavenly desserts.

mini eclairs with vanilla cream

PREPARATION TIME 15 MINUTES • COOKING TIME 30 MINUTES (plus cooling time)

1 teaspoon monounsaturated or polyunsaturated margarine
$1/2$ cup water (125ml)
$1/3$ cup self-raising flour (50g)
2 egg whites
1 tablespoon icing sugar

VANILLA CREAM
200ml low-fat vanilla yogurt
1 teaspoon gelatine
2 teaspoons water

1 Combine margarine and the water in medium saucepan; bring to boil. Add sifted flour all at once, stirring vigorously for about 30 seconds or until smooth. Transfer mixture to small bowl of electric mixer; cool for 5 minutes. Gradually add egg whites, beating well between each addition. Mixture will separate, but will come together with further beating.

2 Spoon mixture into piping bag fitted with 1cm piping tube. Pipe 12 x 5cm thick lengths of mixture onto non-stick oven tray. Bake in hot oven for 10 minutes; reduce heat to moderate. Bake for further 15 minutes or until well browned; cool.

3 When eclairs are cold, cut in half. Scoop out any uncooked mixture; discard. Fill eclairs with vanilla cream; dust with a little sifted icing sugar. Serve with mixed berries, if desired.

Vanilla cream Allow yogurt to come to room temperature. Sprinkle gelatine over the water in cup. Stand in small saucepan of simmering water. Stir until dissolved; cool. Combine yogurt and gelatine mixture in medium bowl; refrigerate until set.

MAKES 12

per eclair 0.6g fat; 172kJ

store Eclairs are best made on day of serving, but do not fill until ready to serve. Unfilled eclairs can be frozen.

custard tarts with low-fat sweet pastry

PREPARATION TIME 20 MINUTES (plus refrigeration time) • COOKING TIME 20 MINUTES (plus cooling time)

1 cup plain flour (150g)
2 tablespoons icing sugar
1 tablespoon custard powder
20g monounsaturated or
   polyunsaturated margarine
1/4 cup cold water
   (60ml), approximately
250g small strawberries, halved
75g blueberries
2 tablespoons diet apricot jam, sieved
2 teaspoons boiling water

CUSTARD FILLING

2 teaspoons gelatine
2 tablespoons water
1 tablespoon caster sugar
1¹/₂ tablespoons custard powder
1 cup skim milk (250ml)
1 teaspoon vanilla essence

1 Place flour, sugar, custard powder and margarine in large bowl of food processor; process until combined. With motor operating, add enough of the water until mixture just begins to form a ball. Knead dough on lightly floured surface until smooth. Cover; refrigerate for 30 minutes. Divide dough into four portions; roll out dough until 5mm thick. Place into four deep 10cm fluted flan tins. Line each pastry case with a piece of baking paper, filled with dried beans or rice; place on oven tray.

2 Bake in moderate oven for about 10 minutes. Remove paper and beans; bake further 10 minutes or until lightly browned. Cool in tins. Remove pastry cases from tins; fill with custard. Refrigerate until custard is set.

3 Arrange berries on top; brush with combined jam and the boiling water.

Custard filling Sprinkle gelatine over the water in cup; stand in small saucepan of simmering water. Stir until dissolved. Combine sugar with custard powder in small saucepan; gradually stir in milk. Stir over heat until mixture boils and thickens. Stir in essence and gelatine mixture.

MAKES 4

per tart 4.1g fat; 1188kJ

store Tarts can be made a day ahead.

apple and pear strudel

PREPARATION TIME 10 MINUTES • COOKING TIME 15 MINUTES (plus cooling time)

1 medium apple (150g)
1 medium pear (230g)
1 tablespoon caster sugar
1/2 teaspoon finely grated
   lemon rind
1/4 teaspoon ground cinnamon
2 tablespoons water
3 sheets fillo pastry

CUSTARD SAUCE

3 teaspoons custard powder
3 teaspoons caster sugar
3/4 cup skim milk (180ml)

1 Peel apple and pear; cut each into quarters. Cut each quarter into three wedges.

2 Combine apple, pear, sugar, rind, cinnamon and the water in large saucepan. Cook until fruit is soft; cool. Layer pastry sheets together; fold in half. Spoon fruit mixture along centre of pastry. Fold in ends; fold sides over fruit.

3 Place strudel, with folded edge underneath, onto baking paper-covered oven tray. Bake in hot oven for about 15 minutes or until well browned. Serve with custard sauce.

Custard sauce Combine custard powder and sugar in medium saucepan; gradually stir in milk. Stir over heat until sauce boils and thickens.

SERVES 2

per serving 0.9g fat; 1123kJ

store Strudel can be prepared a day ahead and refrigerated, covered. Cook just before serving.

apple ginger shortcake

PREPARATION TIME 15 MINUTES (plus refrigeration time)
COOKING TIME 40 MINUTES (plus cooling time)

You will need 1 passionfruit for this recipe.

1¹/₄ cups self-raising flour (185g)
1 tablespoon cornflour
2 tablespoons caster sugar
40g monounsaturated or polyunsaturated margarine
2 egg whites
1 tablespoon lemon juice, approximately
2 tablespoons icing sugar
2 teaspoons ground cinnamon

APPLE GINGER FILLING
425g can pie apples
1 tablespoon passionfruit pulp
1 teaspoon finely chopped glace ginger
1 teaspoon finely grated lemon rind

1 Lightly grease 20cm round sandwich pan; line base with baking paper. Sift flour, cornflour and sugar into large bowl; rub in margarine. Stir in egg whites with enough juice to make ingredients cling together (or process all ingredients until mixture forms a ball). Cover; refrigerate for 30 minutes.

2 Roll three-quarters of the pastry on floured surface until large enough to line base and side of prepared pan.

3 Spread apple ginger filling over base; fold pastry edge over filling. Lightly brush edge with water.

4 Roll out remaining pastry to a 20cm round; place over filling. Press edges to seal.

5 Bake in moderate oven for about 40 minutes or until lightly browned. Cool on wire rack. Sprinkle with combined sifted icing sugar and cinnamon to serve.

Apple ginger filling Combine all ingredients in medium bowl; mix well.

SERVES 8

per serving 3.9g fat; 743J

store Recipe can be made a day ahead and refrigerated, covered.

mango, apple and passionfruit sorbet

PREPARATION TIME 15 MINUTES (plus freezing time) • COOKING TIME 15 MINUTES (plus cooling time)

You will need about 6 passionfruit for this recipe.

1/2 cup caster sugar (110g)
2 cups apple juice (500ml)
1/2 cup water (125ml)
425g can sliced mango in light
 syrup, drained
1/2 cup passionfruit
 pulp (125ml)
4 egg whites

1 Combine sugar, juice and the water in medium saucepan; stir over heat, without boiling, until sugar dissolves. Bring to boil; simmer, uncovered, without stirring, for about 12 minutes or until syrup is thickened slightly (syrup must not change colour); cool.

2 Blend or process mango until smooth. Stir mango and passionfruit into sugar syrup; pour into 20 x 30cm lamington pan. Cover with foil; freeze until just firm.

3 Beat sorbet mixture in small bowl with electric mixer until thick and fluffy; return to pan. Cover; freeze until just firm.

4 Repeat beating process in large bowl; add eggs, one at a time. Beat until fluffy; return mixture to pan. Cover; freeze until firm.

SERVES 4

per serving 0.1g fat; 1704kJ

store Sorbet can be made up to one week ahead.

rich chocolate self-saucing pudding

PREPARATION TIME 15 MINUTES • COOKING TIME 40 MINUTES

cooking oil spray
1 cup self-raising flour (150g)
3/4 cup caster sugar (165g)
2 tablespoons cocoa powder
1/2 cup skim milk (125ml)
1 teaspoon vanilla essence
30g monounsaturated
 or polyunsaturated
 margarine, melted
1/2 cup firmly packed
 brown sugar (100g)
2 tablespoons cocoa powder, extra
1 1/3 cups hot water (330ml)

1 Coat six 3/4 cup capacity dishes with cooking oil spray.

2 Sift flour, caster sugar and cocoa into large bowl. Add combined milk, essence and margarine; stir until smooth. Divide mixture between prepared dishes; sift combined brown sugar and extra cocoa evenly over top.

3 Carefully pour the hot water over each pudding. Bake, uncovered, in moderate oven for about 40 minutes or until puddings are firm. Serve dusted with sifted cocoa powder, if desired.

SERVES 6

per serving 4.6g fat; 1287kJ

store Cook recipe just before serving.

fig and orange pinwheels

PREPARATION TIME 15 MINUTES (plus standing time)
COOKING TIME 20 MINUTES (plus cooling time)

These pinwheels may be drizzled with a simple orange icing if desired, but remember, it will add extra kilojoules.

1³/₄ **cups dried figs (250g), chopped finely**
¹/₄ **cup orange juice (60ml)**
3 cups self-raising flour(450g)
20g monounsaturated or polyunsaturated margarine
1 tablespoon grated orange rind
1 cup skim milk (250ml)
¹/₄ **cup water (60ml), approximately**

1 Combine figs and juice in large bowl; stand for several hours or overnight.

2 Lightly grease deep 23cm round cake pan; line base with baking paper.

3 Sift flour into bowl; rub in margarine. Stir in rind and milk with enough of the water to mix to a firm dough; knead on lightly floured surface until smooth. Roll dough to 20cm x 40cm rectangle. Sprinkle fig mixture evenly over dough. Roll up dough from long side; cut into 12 slices.

4 Place slices in prepared pan; bake in hot oven for about 20 minutes or until cooked through. Stand for 5 minutes before turning onto wire rack to cool.

MAKES 12

per pinwheel 1.8g fat; 820kJ

store Recipe can be made 3 hours ahead and stored in an airtight container, or frozen.

oaty sultana biscuits

PREPARATION TIME 15 MINUTES • COOKING TIME 15 MINUTES (plus cooling time)

1¹/2 cups rolled oats (135g)
¹/2 cup sultanas (80g)
¹/4 cup self-raising flour (75g)
¹/4 cup firmly packed brown
   sugar (50g)
2 egg whites
2 tablespoons honey
20g monounsaturated
   or polyunsaturated
   margarine, melted

1 Combine oats, sultanas, sifted flour and sugar in large bowl. Stir in combined egg whites, honey and margarine.

2 Drop heaped tablespoons of mixture about 3cm apart on baking paper-covered oven trays; press down lightly with fingers.

3 Bake in moderate oven for about 15 minutes or until golden brown. Lift onto wire rack to cool.

MAKES 16

per biscuit 1.6g fat; 392kJ

store Biscuits can be made 3 days ahead and stored in an airtight container.

peach and buttermilk cake

PREPARATION TIME 15 MINUTES • COOKING TIME 45 MINUTES (plus standing time)

2 cups wholemeal self-raising
   flour (320g)
³/4 cup firmly packed
   brown sugar (150g)
2 teaspoons ground cinnamon
1 teaspoon ground ginger
1 egg, beaten lightly
1 egg white, beaten lightly
1 tablespoon monounsaturated
   or polyunsaturated oil
1 cup buttermilk (250ml)
415g can sliced peaches in
   natural juice, drained

1 Lightly grease 20cm sandwich pan; line base with baking paper.

2 Combine flour, sugar, spices, egg, egg white, oil and buttermilk in large bowl. Beat with electric mixer until combined.

3 Spread three-quarters of the mixture into prepared pan. Top with peaches; spread with remaining mixture.

4 Bake in moderate oven for about 45 minutes, or until browned lightly and cooked through. Stand cake for 5 minutes before turning out of pan. Serve cake warm, dusted lightly with sifted icing sugar, if desired.

SERVES 8

per serving 4.2g fat; 849kJ

store Cake is best made close to serving time.

apricot prune loaf

PREPARATION TIME 10 MINUTES (plus standing time) • COOKING TIME 45 MINUTES (plus cooling time)

$^1/_2$ **cup dried apricots (75g)**
1$^1/_4$ cups water (310ml)
1 over-ripe banana
**2 cups wholemeal self-raising
  flour (320g)**
$^1/_4$ **cup caster sugar (55g)**
$^1/_2$ **teaspoon ground cinnamon**
**30g monounsaturated or
  polyunsaturated margarine**
$^1/_2$ **cup pitted prunes (105g),
  chopped finely**
1 egg, beaten lightly

1 Lightly grease 14cm x 21cm loaf pan; line base and two long sides with a strip of baking paper, extending paper 2cm above edge of pan. Combine apricots and the water in medium saucepan; bring to boil. Simmer for 5 minutes; cool to room temperature. Blend or process apricot mixture and banana until smooth.

2 Sift flour, sugar and cinnamon into large bowl; rub in margarine. Stir in prunes, egg and apricot mixture. Spoon mixture into prepared pan.

3 Bake in moderate oven for about 45 minutes or until firm. Stand for 5 minutes before turning onto wire rack to cool.

SERVES 10

per serving 4.1g fat; 914kJ

store Loaf can be made 2 days ahead, and stored in an airtight container, or frozen.

glossary

Some terms, names and alternatives are included here to help everyone to understand and use our recipes perfectly.

Alcohol is optional but gives a particular flavour. You can use fruit juice or water instead to make up the liquid content in our recipes.

All-Bran a low-fat, high-fibre breakfast cereal based on wheat bran.

Allspice ground pimento.

Arrowroot made from starchy extracts from the roots of various tropical plants; used mostly for thickening. Cornflour can be substituted.

Baking paper has a non-stick coating which eliminates the need to grease the paper.

Baking powder a raising agent consisting mainly of 2 parts cream of tartar to 1 part bicarbonate of soda (baking soda).

Barley, rolled grains are rolled flat, similar to rolled oats.

Beans

BLACK fermented, salted and dried soy beans. Use either canned or dried. Chop before, or mash during cooking to release flavour.

BLACK-EYED also known as black-eyed peas.

GREEN French beans.

MEXICANA CHILLI canned pinto beans with chilli flavouring.

Beef

BLADE STEAK cut from the forequarter.

CHUCK STEAK cut from the forequarter.

SCOTCH FILLET rib eye steak.

TOPSIDE STEAK cut from the hindquarter.

Bok choy (Chinese chard) discard stems, use leaves and young tender parts of stems. It requires only a short cooking time.

Bran, unprocessed the outer husk of wheat.

Bread

PITA POCKET unleavened bread which puffs up during cooking, leaving a hollow in the centre.

WHOLEMEAL we used wholewheat sliced bread.

Breadcrumbs

PACKAGED commercially packaged crumbs.

STALE we used 1- or 2-day-old white or wholemeal bread made into crumbs by grating, blending or processing.

BURGHUL

Burghul (cracked wheat) has been cracked by boiling then re-dried.

Capsicum bell pepper.

Cheese

LIGHT MOZZARELLA we used reduced fat mozzarella.

LOW-FAT COTTAGE soft, fresh white cheese made from skim milk.

REDUCED-FAT RICOTTA a low-fat, fresh, unripened cheese made from whey obtained in the manufacture of other cheese.

REDUCED-FAT TASTY natural cheddar cheese.

PARMESAN very hard cheese available grated or by the piece.

Chickpeas also known as garbanzos.

Chicken

BREAST FILLET skinless and boneless.

DRUMSTICK leg.

THIGH FILLET skinless and boneless.

Chillies, fresh available in many different types and sizes. Use rubber gloves when seeding and chopping, as they can burn your skin. Removing seeds and membranes reduces the heat content.

Chilli powder the Asian variety is the hottest and is made from ground red chillies; it can be used as a substitute for fresh chillies in the proportion of 1/2 teaspoon ground chilli powder to 1 medium chilli.

Coleslaw dressing low-oil creamy product.

Cornflour cornstarch.

Cornmeal also called polenta; made from ground corn.

Couscous a fine cereal made from semolina.

Cream, sour light a light, commercially cultured sour cream.

Custard powder pudding mix.

Eggplant aubergine.

Essence, extract.

COFFEE AND CHICORY a slightly bitter syrup based on sugar, caramel, coffee and chicory.

VANILLA we used imitation essence.

Flour

BUCKWHEAT flour milled from buckwheat.

WHITE PLAIN all-purpose flour.

WHITE SELF-RAISING substitute plain (all-purpose) flour and baking powder in the proportion of 3/4 metric cup plain flour to 2 level metric teaspoons baking powder, sift together several times before using. If using an 8oz measuring cup, use 1 cup white plain flour to 2 level metric teaspoons baking powder.

WHOLEMEAL PLAIN wholewheat flour without the addition of baking powder.

WHOLEMEAL SELF-RAISING wholewheat self-raising flour; add baking powder as above to make wholemeal self-raising flour.

Framboise raspberry-flavoured liqueur.

Garam masala varied combinations of cardamom, cinnamon, cloves, coriander, cumin and nutmeg. Sometimes pepper is used to make a hot variation.

Ginger

FRESH, GREEN OR ROOT scrape away skin and it is ready to grate, chop or slice.

GLACE ginger which has been cooked in a heavy sugar syrup, then dried. Crystallised ginger can be substituted for glace ginger; rinse off sugar with water and dry before using.

Grand Marnier an orange-flavoured liqueur.

Herbs we have specified fresh, ground or dried herbs. We used dried (not ground) herbs in the proportion of 1:4 for fresh herbs; for example, 1 teaspoon dried herbs instead of 4 teaspoons chopped fresh herbs.

Just White Egg White Mix a yolk-free, frozen egg substitute available in 300g packets containing three pouches. Each pouch is equivalent to the whites of three large eggs.

Kumara orange sweet potato.

Lamb

CHUMP CHOPS cut from the chump section, between leg and mid-loin.

EGGPLANT

FILLETS very small, lean, tender cut.

Lentils there are many types; all require soaking before cooking, except for red lentils.

Mayonnaise, light use a low-oil product.

Melon, honeydew an oval melon with delicate taste and pale green flesh.

Milk

BUTTERMILK low-fat milk cultured to give a slightly sour, tangy taste; skim milk can be substituted.

SKIM MILK milk from which the butterfat has been almost completely removed.

SKIM MILK POWDER has minimal butterfat.

Noodles, egg are generally sold in compressed bundles and have usually been pre-cooked by steaming so they need only minimal preparation.

Oats, rolled oats with the husks ground off and then steam-softened and rolled flat.

Oil

OLIVE ripe olives are pressed to obtain olive oil. The best oil comes from the first pressing. Two types are marketed, "virgin" and "pure".

POLYUNSATURATED edible vegetable oil.

SPRING ONION

GREEN ONION

WHITE ONION

BROWN ONION

RED ONION

Onions, green known as spring onions and shallots (incorrectly). Do not confuse with the small golden shallots.

Pimientos sweet red capsicum preserved in brine in cans or jars.

Polenta also known as cornmeal.

Polyunsaturated margarine made from polyunsaturated fats found in vegetable oils. Flavourings, colours and vitamins A and D are usually added.

Pork

BUTTERFLY STEAK skinless, boneless mid-loin chop which has been split and opened out flat.

FILLET skinless, boneless eye-fillet from the loin.

MEDALLION eye of the loin.

Pumpkin any type of pumpkin can be substituted for butternut or golden nugget.

Rice can be brown or white.

BASMATI a delicately flavoured rice from Pakistan; white long grain rice can be substituted.

RED a long-grain type of rice with red husks available from Asian food stores.

RICE CAKE light and crunchy wholegrain crispbread made from rice, corn and water (a gluten-free and wheat-free product).

WILD from North America, not a member of the rice family; it is expensive as it is difficult to cultivate but has a distinctive flavour.

Sauce

CHILLI we used a hot Chinese variety. It consists of chillies, salt and vinegar. We used it sparingly so increase the amounts in recipes to suit your taste.

CRANBERRY cranberries preserved in sugar syrup; has an astringent flavour.

FISH made from the liquid drained from salted, fermented anchovies. It has a strong smell and taste. Use sparingly until you acquire the taste.

OYSTER a rich, brown bottled sauce made from oysters cooked in salt and soy sauce.

SOY made from fermented soy beans. The light variety is generally used with white meat dishes for flavour, and the darker variety with red meat dishes for colour.

SWEET CHILLI a piquant mix of sugar, chilli, vinegar, salt and spices; use sparingly.

TABASCO made with vinegar, hot red peppers and salt; use sparingly.

TOMATO tomato ketchup, we used a variety with no added salt.

Sambal oelek also spelt ulek and olek, is a paste made from chillies and salt. Use as an ingredient or accompaniment.

Semolina a cereal made from hard durum wheat. Used in puddings, cakes, desserts and some savoury dishes.

Snow peas small flat pods with tiny barely formed peas inside. They are eaten whole, pod and all. They require only a short cooking time.

Spice, Chinese assorted packaged mixed spices.

Spinach

ENGLISH a soft-leafed vegetable, more delicate in taste than silverbeet, young, tender silverbeet leaves can be substituted for English spinach.

SILVERBEET a large-leafed vegetable; remove course white stems, cook green leafy parts.

Stock cube 1 stock cube is equivalent to 1 teaspoon powdered bouillon.

Stuffing mix, seasoned a tasty packaged mix containing breadcrumbs and flavourings.

Sultanas dried seedless grapes; also known as white raisins.

Sugar

CASTER fine granulated table sugar.

CRYSTAL coarse granulated table sugar.

ICING confectioners' sugar.

Syrup

CORN available in light or dark; either can be used.

GOLDEN a by-product of sugar; honey can usually be substituted.

GRENADINE non-alcoholic flavouring made from pomegranate juice, bright red in colour. Imitation cordial is also available.

MAPLE we used dark amber maple syrup. Pancake syrup, golden syrup or honey can usually be substituted.

Tahini paste made from crushed sesame seeds.

Tangerine a variety of mandarin with deeper, orange-red skin which is easily peeled, generally very sweet and juicy.

Tempeh is produced by a natural culture of soy beans; has a chunky, chewy texture.

Tofu also known as bean curd; made similarly to cheese, but from soy bean "milk". We used both soft and firm fresh tofu.

WILD RICE

Tomato

PASTE a concentrated tomato puree used in flavouring soups, stews, sauces etc. We used a variety with no added salt.

PUREE canned pureed tomatoes.

TOMATOES, CANNED we used a variety with no added salt.

Veal

NUT OF VEAL a solid piece of meat off the leg.

MEDALLION eye of the loin.

Vermouth a wine flavoured with a number of different herbs and generally used as an aperitif and in cocktails.

Vinegar

CIDER VINEGAR made from fermented apples.

RED WINE VINEGAR is made from red wine by a slow process, flavoured with herbs and spices; it is strongly aromatic.

WHITE WINE VINEGAR made from white wine, flavoured with herbs, spices and fruit.

Wholemeal wholewheat.

Wine we used good quality dry red and dry white wines. For a sweet white wine in a dessert, we used a moselle.

Green ginger wine an Australian sweet white wine infused with crushed fresh ginger.

Wrappers

GOW GEE WRAPPERS OR PASTRY are sold frozen, thaw before using; keep covered with a damp cloth while using.

SPRING ROLL WRAPPERS OR PASTRY are sold frozen, thaw before using; keep covered with a damp cloth while using.

Yeast allow 3 teaspoons (7g) dried granulated yeast to 15g compressed (fresh) yeast.

Yogurt, low-fat plain unflavoured yogurt.

Zucchini courgette.

index

make your own stock

These recipes can be made up to 4 days ahead and stored, covered, in the refrigerator. Be sure to remove any fat from the surface after the cooled stock has been refrigerated overnight. If the stock is to be kept longer, it is best to freeze it in smaller quantities. *All stock recipes make about 2.5 litres (10 cups).*

Stock is also available in cans or tetra packs. Stock cubes or powder can be used. As a guide, 1 teaspoon of stock powder or 1 small crumbled stock cube mixed with 1-cup (250ml) water will give a fairly strong stock. Be aware of the salt and fat content of stock cubes and powders and prepared stocks.

BEEF STOCK

2kg meaty beef bones
2 medium onions (300g)
2 sticks celery, chopped
2 medium carrots (250g), chopped
3 bay leaves
2 teaspoons black peppercorns
5 litres (20 cups) water
3 litres (12 cups) water, extra

Place bones and unpeeled chopped onions in baking dish. Bake in hot oven about 1-hour or until bones and onions are well browned. Transfer bones and onions to large pan, add celery, carrots, bay leaves, peppercorns and water, simmer, uncovered, 3 hours. Add extra water, simmer, uncovered, further 1 hour; strain.

CHICKEN STOCK

2kg chicken bones
2 medium onions (300g), chopped
2 sticks celery, chopped
2 medium carrots (250g), chopped
3 bay leaves
2 teaspoons black peppercorns
5 litres (20 cups) water

Combine all ingredients in large pan, simmer, uncovered, 2 hours; strain.

FISH STOCK

1.5kg fish bones
3 litres (12 cups) water
1 medium onion (150g), chopped
2 sticks celery, chopped
2 bay leaves
1 teaspoon black peppercorns

Combine all ingredients in large pan, simmer, uncovered, 20 minutes; strain.

VEGETABLE STOCK

2 large carrots (360g), chopped
2 large parsnips (360g), chopped
4 medium onions (600g), chopped
12 sticks celery, chopped
4 bay leaves
2 teaspoons black peppercorns
6 litres (24 cups) water

Combine all ingredients in large pan, simmer, uncovered, 1½ hours; strain.

conversion chart

MEASURES

One Australian metric measuring cup holds approximately 250ml; one Australian metric tablespoon holds 20ml; one Australian metric teaspoon holds 5ml.

The difference between one country's measuring cups and another's is within a two- or three-teaspoon variance, and will not affect your cooking results. North America, New Zealand and the United Kingdom use a 15ml tablespoon.

All cup and spoon measurements are level. The most accurate way of measuring dry ingredients is to weigh them. When measuring liquids, use a clear glass or plastic jug with the metric markings.

We use large eggs with an average weight of 60g.

DRY MEASURES

METRIC	IMPERIAL
15g	½oz
30g	1oz
60g	2oz
90g	3oz
125g	4oz (¼lb)
155g	5oz
185g	6oz
220g	7oz
250g	8oz (½lb)
280g	9oz
315g	10oz
345g	11oz
375g	12oz (¾lb)
410g	13oz
440g	14oz
470g	15oz
500g	16oz (1lb)
750g	24oz (1½lb)
1kg	32oz (2lb)

LIQUID MEASURES

METRIC	IMPERIAL
30ml	1 fluid oz
60ml	2 fluid oz
100ml	3 fluid oz
125ml	4 fluid oz
150ml	5 fluid oz (¼ pint/1 gill)
190ml	6 fluid oz
250ml	8 fluid oz
300ml	10 fluid oz (½ pint)
500ml	16 fluid oz
600ml	20 fluid oz (1 pint)
1000ml (1 litre)	1¾ pints

LENGTH MEASURES

METRIC	IMPERIAL
3mm	⅛in
6mm	¼in
1cm	½in
2cm	¾in
2.5cm	1in
5cm	2in
6cm	2½in
8cm	3in
10cm	4in
13cm	5in
15cm	6in
18cm	7in
20cm	8in
23cm	9in
25cm	10in
28cm	11in
30cm	12in (1ft)

OVEN TEMPERATURES

These oven temperatures are only a guide for conventional ovens. For fan-forced ovens, check the manufacturer's manual.

	°C (CELSIUS)	°F (FAHRENHEIT)	GAS MARK
Very slow	120	250	½
Slow	150	275-300	1-2
Moderately slow	170	325	3
Moderate	180	350-375	4-5
Moderately hot	200	400	6
Hot	220	425-450	7-8
Very hot	240	475	9

ARE YOU MISSING SOME OF THE WORLD'S FAVOURITE COOKBOOKS?

The Australian Women's Weekly Cookbooks are available from bookshops, cookshops, supermarkets and other stores all over the world. You can also buy direct from the publisher, using the order form below.

TITLE	RRP	QTY	TITLE	RRP	QTY
Asian Meals in Minutes	£6.99		Great Lamb Cookbook	£6.99	
Babies & Toddlers Good Food	£6.99		Greek Cooking Class	£6.99	
Barbecue Meals In Minutes	£6.99		Healthy Heart Cookbook	£6.99	
Basic Cooking Class	£6.99		Indian Cooking Class	£6.99	
Beginners Cooking Class	£6.99		Japanese Cooking Class	£6.99	
Beginners Simple Meals	£6.99		Kids' Birthday Cakes	£6.99	
Beginners Thai	£6.99		Kids Cooking	£6.99	
Best Food	£6.99		Lean Food	£6.99	
Best Food Desserts	£6.99		Low-carb, Low-fat	£6.99	
Best Food Fast	£6.99		Low-fat Feasts	£6.99	
Best Food Mains	£6.99		Low-fat Food For Life	£6.99	
Cakes, Biscuits & Slices	£6.99		Low-fat Meals in Minutes	£6.99	
Cakes Cooking Class	£6.99		Main Course Salads	£6.99	
Caribbean Cooking	£6.99		Middle Eastern Cooking Class	£6.99	
Casseroles	£6.99		Midweek Meals in Minutes	£6.99	
Chicken	£6.99		Muffins, Scones & Breads	£6.99	
Chicken Meals in Minutes	£6.99		New Casseroles	£6.99	
Chinese Cooking Class	£6.99		New Classics	£6.99	
Christmas Cooking	£6.99		New Finger Food	£6.99	
Chocolate	£6.99		Party Food and Drink	£6.99	
Cocktails	£6.99		Pasta Meals in Minutes	£6.99	
Cooking for Friends	£6.99		Potatoes	£6.99	
Creative Cooking on a Budget	£6.99		Salads: Simple, Fast & Fresh	£6.99	
Detox	£6.99		Saucery	£6.99	
Dinner Beef	£6.99		Sauces, Salsas & Dressings (May '06)	£6.99	
Dinner Lamb	£6.99		Sensational Stir-Fries	£6.99	
Dinner Seafood	£6.99		Short-order Cook	£6.99	
Easy Australian Style	£6.99		Slim	£6.99	
Easy Curry	£6.99		Sweet Old-Fashioned Favourites	£6.99	
Easy Spanish-Style	£6.99		Thai Cooking Class	£6.99	
Essential Soup	£6.99		Vegetarian Meals in Minutes	£6.99	
Freezer, Meals from the	£6.99		Vegie Food	£6.99	
French Food, New	£6.99		Weekend Cook	£6.99	
Fresh Food for Babies & Toddlers	£6.99		Wicked Sweet Indulgences	£6.99	
Get Real, Make a Meal	£6.99		Wok Meals in Minutes	£6.99	
Good Food Fast	£6.99		TOTAL COST:	£	

ACP Magazines Ltd Privacy Notice
This book may contain offers, competitions or surveys that require you to provide information about yourself if you choose to enter or take part in any such Reader Offer. If you provide information about yourself to ACP Magazines Ltd, the company will use this information to provide you with the products or services you have requested, and may supply your information to contractors that help ACP to do this. ACP will also use your information to inform you of other ACP publications, products, services and events. ACP will also give your information to organisations that are providing special prizes or offers, and that are clearly associated with the Reader Offer. Unless you tell us not to, we may give your information to other organisations that use it to inform you about other products, services and events or who may give it to other organisations that may use it for this purpose. If you would like to gain access to the information ACP holds about you, please contact ACP's Privacy Officer at ACP Magazines Ltd, 54-58 Park Street, Sydney, NSW 2000.

☐ **Privacy Notice**
Please do not provide information about me to any organisation not associated with this offer.

Mr/Mrs/Ms _____

Address _____

_____ Postcode _____

Day time phone _____ Email* (optional) _____

I enclose my cheque/money order for £ _____

or please charge £ _____

to my: ☐ Access ☐ Mastercard ☐ Visa ☐ Diners Club

PLEASE NOTE: WE DO NOT ACCEPT SWITCH OR ELECTRON CARDS

Card number ☐☐☐☐ ☐☐☐☐ ☐☐☐☐ ☐☐☐☐

Expiry date _____ 3 digit security code *(found on reverse of card)* _____

Cardholder's name_____ Signature _____

To order: Mail or fax – photocopy or complete the order form above, and send your credit card details or cheque payable to: Australian Consolidated Press (UK), Moulton Park Business Centre, Red House Road, Moulton Park, Northampton NN3 6AQ, phone (+44) (0) 1604 497531 fax (+44) (0) 1604 497533, e-mail books@acpmedia.co.uk or order online at www.acpuk.com

Non-UK residents: We accept the credit cards listed on the coupon, or cheques, drafts or International Money Orders payable in sterling and drawn on a UK bank. Credit card charges are at the exchange rate current at the time of payment.

Postage and packing UK: Add £1.00 per order plus 50p per book.

Postage and packing overseas: Add £2.00 per order plus £1.00 per book.

All pricing current at time of going to press and subject to change/availability.

Offer ends 31.12.2006

* By including your email address, you consent to receipt of any email regarding this magazine, and other emails which inform you of ACP's other publications, products, services and events, and to promote third party goods and services you may be interested in.